HONEST PRETZELS

AND 64 OTHER AMAZING RECIPES
FOR COOKS AGES 8 & UP

WRITTEN AND ILLUSTRATED BY
MOLLIE KATZEN

TRICYCLE PRESS
BERKELEY, CALIFORNIA

TO MY DAUGHTER, EVE, WITH DELICIOUS LOVE

CONVERSIONS

Temperature:

400° F	= 200° C	= gas mark 6
375° F	= 190° C	= gas mark 5

Length:

1 inch	= 2.5 cm
6 inches	= 15.24 cm
12 inches	= 30.48 cm

Dry:

1 teaspoon			= 5 g
1/4 cup	= 4 tbs	= 2 oz	= 60 g
1 cup	= 1/2 pound	= 8 oz	= 250 g

Liquid:

1/4 cup	= 2 fl oz	= 60 ml
1 cup	= 8 fl oz	= 250 ml
1 ounce (British) = .96 oz (U.S.)		

Butter:

1/8 cup	= 2 tbs	= 1 oz	= 30 g
1/4 cup	= 4 tbs	= 2 oz (1/2 stick)	= 55 g
1/2 cup	= 8 tbs	= 4 oz (1 stick)	= 110 g

All-Purpose Flour:

1 cup	= 5 oz	= 140 g
1/2 cup	= 2 1/2 oz	= 70 g

Miscellaneous:

applesauce	= stewed apple
baking soda	= bicarbonate of soda
bell pepper	= capsicum
cornmeal	= maize flour
cornstarch	= cornflour
flour, bread	= strong flour
flour, unbleached	= plain flour
green bean	= french bean
heavy cream	= double cream
jack cheese	= mild white melting cheese
peanut	= groundnut
plastic wrap	= cling film
powdered sugar	= icing sugar
raisins	= sultanas
rolled oats	= oat flakes
skillet	= frying pan
spatula	= fish slice
zucchini	= courgette

We have taken great care to highlight safety, but cannot emphasize too much that anyone working in the kitchen with children must pay careful attention, as there are potential risks. Neither the author nor the publisher assumes responsibility for any accident or misadventure resulting from the use of this book.

 TRICYCLE PRESS
P.O. Box 7123, Berkeley, California 94707
www.tenspeed.com

Book design by Mollie Katzen and Nancy Austin
Typeset in Goudy Sans, Stone Serif, and Stone Sans

Library of Congress Cataloging-in-Publication Data

Katzen, Mollie, 1950–
   Honest pretzels: and 64 other amazing recipes for cooks ages 8 & up / Mollie Katzen
     p. cm.
   Summary: Provides step-by-step instructions for a variety of recipes, arranged in such categories as "Breakfast Specials," "Soups, Sandwiches & Salads for Lunch or Dinner," and "Desserts and a Few Baked Things."
   ISBN 1-883672-88-0
   1. Pretzels Juvenile literature. 2. Cookery Juvenile literature.
[1. Cookery.] I. Title
TX770.P73K38 1999
641.5'123—dc21   99–20184
                                    CIP

First printing, 1999
Printed in Singapore

1 2 3 4 5 6 7 - 03 02 01 00 99

ACKNOWLEDGMENTS

I want to express my gratitude to all of the wonderful people who helped me with this book in many ways:

My two children and resident focus group, Sam and Eve, who have been my primary sources of inspiration, as well as models, art critics, recipe testers, and morale boosters;

My husband Carl, for constant support and nourishment of my "process";

Maureen Collins, who greatly assisted with the recipe tests;

Nicole Geiger, editor extraordinaire, who went many extra miles to keep this project on track;

Nancy Austin, super book designer, upon whose taste and expertise I totally rely;

Torri Randall, a heaven-sent one-woman author support squad;

Suzanne Sherman, fabulous copy editor;

Nancy Ropecka, fastest keyboarder in the West;

Barbara King, eagle-eyed proofreader;

Cybele Knowles, Christine Longmuir, Amy Cleary, Mary Ann Anderson, and Andrea Flint—the Tricycle Press dream team;

Phil Wood and Kirsty Melville—the Ten Speed Press honchos, who have consistently honored me with their faith and trust;

Kate Heyhoe, doyenne of culinary knowledge and communication, and Michele Anna Jordan, esteemed colleague and friend—great personal cheerleaders;

Ken Swezey, legal guru and business visionary;

Abe Katzen, Eli Katzen, Stewart Katzen, William Von Hoene, Branden Zollar, and Lia Jakubowitz: high-level advisors on the culinary tastes of juveniles;

Noah Isaacs, Yaeir Heber, Arie Levine, Emily Karwat, Amy Mayper, Karina Piser, Tali and Ariel Stachel Yeshayahu, Rachel Weiss, Chelsea Elliott, Heather Alarab, Laura Gorrin, Izzi and Sophia Blachman-Biatch, Susie Ashkenaz, Stefan and Jesse Goldberg, Megan Winkleman, Elizabeth Carlen, Irene and Zach Hamaker, Liat and Shani Litwin, Kyle Miller, and Zachary Morfin: recipe testers par excellence. Thanks to all of you—plus the many other children who have cooked with me over the years—and to your parents for loaning you to this project.

CONTENTS

HI, KIDS!

This cookbook is for *you*. It will teach you how to make a lot of great food to share with your family and friends. And while you're cooking, you can have a whole bunch of fun!

You are mostly the boss of these recipes. An adult must be there, aware of what you are doing, and available to set up and help. But *you* are the one who will read the recipes and be the leader of what happens. It's like you (and maybe some of your friends) and an adult are a team, and the kids get to be in charge.

Look through the book to see which recipes seem interesting, then ask your parents for permission to make whatever you choose. Read the first part of the instructions together to find out what the ingredients are and how to set up. (It is actually more fun to cook when everything is all set up ahead of time.)

The next part of each recipe shows the actual cooking steps, which are on the pages with little boxes that have writing and some pictures inside. You can follow these instructions yourself. Read the recipe all the way through first, and then get busy. Pretty soon you'll feel like an actual chef, making all sorts of main dishes, side dishes, desserts, snacks, and drinks—for real!

If there are any parts of cooking (handling sharp knives, hot stove, oven, blender) that you feel uncomfortable with, be sure to ask an adult to give you a hand. You don't have to push yourself to be readier than you are.

Have the *best* time becoming the world's most fantastic cook! I wish I could be there with you to taste everything you make.

Love,

Mollie Katzen

P.S. When you are finished reading this page, please give the book to a parent or adult cooking partner. I wrote the next part for them.

TO THE ADULT

For many adults the thought of kids in the kitchen brings up dreaded images of spaghetti sauce dripping from the ceiling, pudding wallpaper, and eggshell battlefields with no survivors. I used to think this way myself until about ten years ago, when I plunged head-on into the shared adult-child cooking experience. I found out some very good news: cooking with children can be an absolutely wonderful, eye-opening experience for the adult as well as for the child.

How did this awareness come about? Intrigued by my then-toddler son's enthusiasm for his weekly preschool cooking session (the sheer existence of which was a revelation to me), I started going into the classroom to watch. I was tremendously moved to witness the passion with which these very little children (ages three through five) approached every detail of food preparation. I was struck by how they rose to the occasion and could (and *did*) earnestly concentrate when allowed to really get involved in the project at hand. Soon afterward, I spent some time in the preschool running the cooking classes in collaboration with the classroom teacher, Ann Henderson. Those lessons eventually evolved into a cookbook for preschoolers, called *Pretend Soup and Other Real Recipes* (Tricycle Press, 1994).

Inspired to give it a try at home, I have now been cooking with children—my own and many of their friends and schoolmates—ever since. Of course, my children have gotten older and matured, and their experience and appreciation of cooking has deepened. As their reading, math, science, and logic skills have developed, and their physical coordination has become more refined, I have felt a need for a cookbook that speaks to them and to other children in the middle age range (eight years old and up). With this mission as a guiding force, I have spent the past few years working with grade school– and middle school–aged children to create *Honest Pretzels*.

The goal of this book is to address a more sophisticated palate, a broader interest level, and a more mature set of skills—to pick up where *Pretend Soup* leaves off. While writing *Honest Pretzels,* I have enjoyed the wonderful privilege of learning firsthand what cooking means to kids. It means a great deal! But don't just take my word for it. Open up your kitchen to your children, let them lead you through the recipes in these pages, and make the leap. I think you'll be glad you did.

WHAT KIDS GET OUT OF COOKING

- A blossoming of creativity and a sense of aesthetics, fun, and sensuality

- Confidence and self-esteem; a feeling of accomplishment

- Math skills (addition, logic, fractions, spatial geometry, multiplication)

- Reading comprehension skills

- Sequencing skills and development of logical thinking

- Communication and organization skills; a sense of teamwork and bonding with parent-helpers, siblings, and friends

- Refinement of small motor skills and hand–eye coordination

- Science skills (chemistry, physics, cause and effect)

- Cultural awareness from trying different ethnic cooking styles

- Language skills (observing, describing, predicting outcomes)

- Sense of responsibility: following directions and delegating tasks

- Sense of time; patience skills

- Food literacy (openness to trying new foods, and subsequent appreciation and awareness; familiarity with ingredients, techniques, processes)

- Increased interest in and curiosity about all of the above

THE "CUISINE"

This book is organized into five chapters, which include child-tested (and approved) recipes for breakfast, lunch, dinner, desserts, snacks, drinks, and a few baked goods. I don't expect children in this age group to be making entire family meals by themselves, but rather to *participate* in meal preparation in a significant way. The recipes are all vegetarian, so that children who prefer not to eat meat can partake of everything. But kids who love their chicken and burgers are also going to be excited by this food. An important goal is to give children the chance to become more familiar with—and appreciative of—fresh fruit and vegetables *on their own terms*, and not just to please their parents.

THE COOKING SKILLS

Some of the skills your child will learn from these pages:

- Making and handling yeasted dough

- Making filled, shaped, healthy pastries

- Slicing, mincing, and grating

- Seasoning with herbs and spices

- Sautéing, puréeing, measuring, layering, assembling

- Dividing, estimating, timing, deciding (judgment calls)

- Separating eggs, beating egg whites, folding a puffy batter

- Making simple, standard sauces

- Basic kitchen safety and common sense

Along the way, your children will also become knowledgeable about flavor (with recipes like Mysterious Dipping Sauce and Ranch Dressing) and texture (with others like Homemade Tortilla Chips). They will learn about the components of common foods when they make Little Pizzas and Honest Pretzels, and they'll get a subtle lesson in healthier food choices with Cool Shakes, Excellent Soda, and Healthy Snack Ideas.

HOW TO BE AN ASSISTANT TO YOUR CHILD AND WORK AS A TEAM

As much as possible, let your child select what to make, and then be on hand to give final approval. Review and read through everything together before you start. Every recipe is preceded by a page or two of introduction, with complete lists for the ingredients and tools that will be needed. If any advance preparation is required, these pages will let you and your child know what to do. For the purposes of safety, there is also a list of tasks that, in most cases, will require adult assistance. When you go over these preliminary pages together, make sure you have a good understanding of what is about to happen and who is doing what. Don't be surprised if your child wants you to assist with more steps than the instructions suggest. It's a personal matter, and it is good for a child to know—and heed—his or her comfort level with various tasks.

Once the cooking has begun, be sure to let your child be the "leader-reader" of the actual steps.

WORKING WITH MORE THAN ONE CHILD

If several children want to cook together, it is important that they be good cooperators, otherwise, you could have a crowd-control problem on your hands, with everyone competing to do all of the fun tasks. It's a good idea to have one child be the designated recipe reader and the other be the doer. Then they can trade off.

If there are younger children hanging around who want to "help" but are not quite ready to make these recipes, here are some tasks to keep them happy and out of the big kids' hair: washing vegetables, setting the table, making decorations for the table, "painting" melted butter or oil into the pan, mashing things (bananas, avocados), sprinkling grated cheese, playing with an extra piece of dough. Little kids also love to pat batters into pans, so hand over a wooden spoon and let them pat away. It's nice not to have to shoo away the younger kids, so they can be around to absorb the positive energy of cooking. (You can also promise younger children a cooking session of their own later on, from *Pretend Soup*.)

SETTING UP

Setting up is an important part of cooking. The more organized, the more relaxed and enjoyable the experience will be for all involved. Always help your child with—and oversee—the set-up. If you are concerned about messes, put a plastic tablecloth or placemats underneath the work area. Have paper towels (plus a damp rag for wiping hands) nearby.

TIPS FOR SETTING UP

- Make sure the work level is appropriate to your child's height, and that the preparations are appropriate for his or her strength and motor skills. This will not only make the project safer but more enjoyable. I find that for kids in this age range it is ideal to work standing up at a kitchen or dining room table, especially when handling dough.

- Consider purchasing an electric frying pan or a set of portable electric burners for your child. This can be set up on a table at a child-friendly height and used for most of the stovetop dishes in the book. Remember that when cooking is brought down to a more comfortable (reachable, watchable) level, kids can see and do more, learn more, and gain more confidence.

- It's easier to measure flour, sugar, corn-meal, and other dry ingredients by dipping a measuring cup into a big bin or container and then leveling it off than it is to try to pour these ingredients out. An oversized, wide-mouthed glass jar is the ideal storage unit for dry ingredients. Set up the flour-measuring station on a tray to catch spills.

- It's always better for a mixing bowl to be too large than too small. This way, your child can mix enthusiastically and thoroughly without sending batter flying across the room.

STREAMLINING THE PROCESS

Certain time-consuming (or daunting) tasks, such as chopping onions, mincing garlic, or grating cheese, can sometimes inhibit the cooking process. If any of these jobs is an issue for your child, consider the following:

- Keep whole, peeled onions in the freezer. Cut them into quarters and either let the kids finish the job, or do it yourself. A bonus here is that frozen onions will not make you cry.

- You can also keep *chopped* onions in the freezer. To freeze chopped onions, cut a bunch, spread them out on a tray in the freezer until solid, and then repack them in a sealed plastic freezer bag. Store them in a reachable spot in the freezer for easy access. No defrosting is necessary; just scoop them out and use as needed. (They will keep in the freezer for about a month.)

- You can give grated cheese the same freezer treatment as chopped onions (see above). Grate a quantity, spread it out on a tray to freeze it so the pieces stay separate, and then repack it in a sealed plastic bag and store in the freezer for up to a month.

- Mince a lot of garlic at a time. (A great tool for this is a mini food processor, with about a 1-cup capacity.) Store the garlic in a tightly closed jar in the refrigerator, so your child can just reach in with a measuring spoon and use it as needed. (It will keep in the refrigerator for about 5 days.)

- Cut fruit or vegetables into larger chunks first, and then let your young chef do the final slicing or chopping.

- Read through the set-up steps to determine which tasks can be done ahead of time (like cooking the rice for Vegetarian Fried Rice or boiling and draining the pasta for Not-from-a-Box Macaroni and Cheese).

- Keep a sinkful of warm, sudsy water on hand to soak used dishes as you go.

AWARENESS OF TIME

Cooking is largely about time. Have a clock with a minute hand and a timer with a bell close by as part of the regular set-up.

There is no hurried step in any of these recipes. Remind the children to take their time. This keeps things neater and safer. Try to schedule cooking projects when there is plenty of time to set up, cook, eat, and clean up. Haste really does make waste. Not only that, it also makes bummers.

Since waiting is a challenge to children of any age, encourage them to plan some activities to do (like card tricks, a board game, or drawing pictures of the food) while they wait. Have the supplies close by so the kids won't wander off and lose their connection to the project at hand. If they do go off to another area of the house, have them take the timer with them, so they can be the ones responsible for keeping track of the cooking or baking process.

SAFETY ISSUES

Always be on the premises, aware of the cooking project, and available to help. As I've already mentioned (but it bears repeating!), these recipes instruct the kids to consult with an adult before beginning the cooking project, and to get help with ingredient gathering and set-up. (There are also steps within the recipes that remind the child to ask for adult help with specific tasks.)

Be very clear about the safety rules in your household. State them calmly, and also make a safety rules list with your child to hang on the wall so everyone can memorize it. After a while, as your child becomes more adept and comfortable in the kitchen, these rules will become second nature.

Make sure all kids in this age range who cook in your house are thoroughly acquainted with the stove (or electric skillet). They should be familiar with "high," "medium," and "low" settings. If you use an electric burner, train your child to understand that the burner stays hot for some time even after it is turned off (and to ask for help moving heavier pots off any burner).

BASIC ADULT JOBS

- Being there and being aware

- Making sure hands are washed before beginning

- Seeing to it that all of the kids are wearing short sleeves and that long hair is tied back or otherwise restrained

- Putting things in or taking them out of an oven

- Handling hot, melted butter—whether it's coming out of a microwave or from a pot on the stovetop

- Handling any knife larger than a paring knife

- Setting up the food processor or electric mixer

- Taking any and all food out of a food processor

- Scraping food out of a blender (A child eight years old or older may pour.)

- Helping with *anything* a child feels uncomfortable or unsafe doing alone!

TAKING IT FURTHER

Now that you've kindled your child's interest in cooking, you can sustain and nurture it with field trips and related activities.

- Visit farmers' markets, green grocers, bakeries, gardens, and orchards.

- Read and discuss books about food in various cultures—and about agriculture.

- Buy your child a blank, bound journal so she can record her responses to the recipes, new ideas, and more. This can be the beginning of her own personal cookbook!

- Give your child a special pad of paper to make his own shopping lists, and give him a folder to store these in. He can keep track of what he's cooked and can refer to his own "files" the next time around.

- Encourage familiarity with the kitchen. Give your child projects to be in charge of, like certain inventories (rice, beans, raisins, sugar). Collect glass jars with lids so she can help fill them and keep track of them. Buy a set of labels your child can decorate and use on the jars.

This book is designed to stimulate children's curiosity and to let them be in charge and feel genuinely useful. The exciting goals here are for children to gain independence within the confines of a safe environment and to work in collaboration with an adult, but with the roles reversed: the child is the executive chef and the adult is the sous chef. This requires some letting go on your part, and a lot of faith. The benefits will be great, as you are about to discover!

"I'm gonna like it because I made it!" —Eve

CHAPTER 1

BREAKFAST SPECIALS

GINGERBREAD FRENCH TOAST

One of the kids who tested this recipe wanted to know if we would get to make French toast out of actual gingerbread. That does sound good, but if we soaked gingerbread in the batter it would turn to mush and you'd have a big mess instead of breakfast. To make something just as delicious, we add gingerbread spices (cinnamon, ginger, and allspice) to the batter. Then we put in some bread to soak up all the flavor. It's almost like having dessert for breakfast!

INGREDIENTS:

- 2 eggs
- 1/2 cup milk
- 1 teaspoon cinnamon
- 1 teaspoon powdered ginger
- 1/4 teaspoon allspice
- 3 or 4 slices Italian or sourdough bread, or challah (egg bread)
- A slice or 2 of butter for the pan

TO PUT ON TOP (YOU CHOOSE):

- Real maple syrup
- Applesauce
- Sliced peaches or strawberries
- Powdered sugar

YIELD: This recipe makes 3 or 4 servings.

TIME: It takes about 25 minutes to make and cook, start to finish.

YOU WILL ALSO NEED:

- Small bowl for breaking the eggs
- 2-cup liquid measure
- Whisk
- Pie pan
- Fork for dipping bread
- Dinner knife for cutting butter
- Frying pan
- Spatula
- Plates and forks

Should you ask an adult for help?

That's up to you, but make sure there is an adult in the house who knows you are doing this and can help you set up. (And, of course, if there is any task you feel uncomfortable doing, ask for help.)

1

Break 2 **eggs** into a bowl.

2

Pour the **milk** into a 2-cup measuring cup until it reaches the line for $1/2$ cup. Add to the milk:

the eggs

1 teaspoon **cinnamon**

1 teaspoon **ginger**

$1/4$ teaspoon **allspice**

Whisk until it is all one color.

3

Pour the mixture into a pie pan.

Use a fork or your hands to dip a slice of **bread** on both sides until it is soaked. Put the wet bread on a plate for now. Do this with all of the bread.

4

Put a frying pan on the stove and turn on the heat to **medium**.

4 1/2

Use a dinner knife to slice some **butter**. Put it in the pan and push it around until it is melted all over the inside of the pan.

5

Put the wet bread in the hot pan and cook until it is brown underneath. (Use a spatula to peek.) Flip the bread with the spatula and cook on the other side until brown.

6

Serve hot—plain, or with **syrup** or **fruit**, or **powdered sugar** sprinkled on top.

TIME TO EAT!

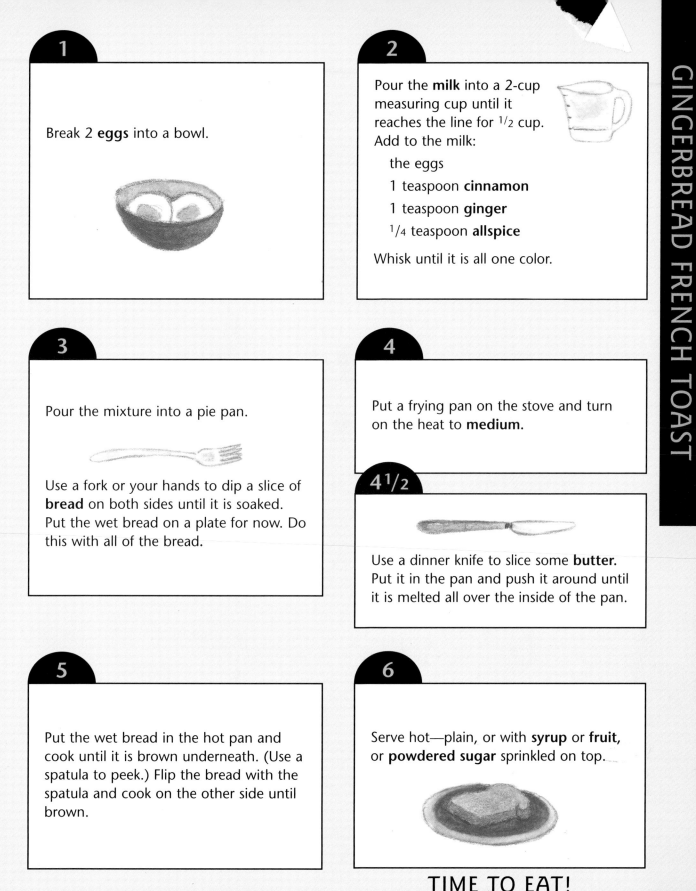

Your Favorite Yogurt Pancakes

These are called "Your Favorite Yogurt Pancakes" because you get to make them with *your* favorite flavor of yogurt. The flavor of the yogurt becomes the flavor of the pancakes.

If you are using the kind of yogurt where you have to mix in the fruit from the bottom of the container, go ahead and mix it with a spoon ahead of time, the same as if you were about to eat it. But, instead of eating it, you will put all of the yogurt right into the pancake batter! It might sound silly, but it really works. In most cases, little containers of yogurt contain eight ounces, which equals exactly 1 cup, the amount needed for this recipe. So, if you are using one of those containers that says "Net Weight 8 Ounces" on the bottom of the label, you don't have to measure it for this recipe. But scoop the whole cup of yogurt into the 2-cup liquid measure anyway because you will add the milk, butter, and egg to it and then mix everything together right in the cup (as we do with a lot of these recipes). Mixing right in the cup is very convenient, and it saves on clean-up.

If you don't use up all of the pancake batter, put it in a container with a cover and store it in the refrigerator for up to two days. You can cook the rest another day. When the batter is made ahead of time, you might even be able to cook some pancakes for yourself on a school morning, for extra cheer. (Of course, make sure this is okay with your parents.)

"When you put them in the pan, they get wider." —Jenny

"It's good even without syrup." —Adam

INGREDIENTS:

- 1 cup unbleached white flour
- $^1/_2$ teaspoon salt
- 1 teaspoon baking powder
- 1 tablespoon butter for the batter, plus a little more for the pan
- 1 cup flavored yogurt (your choice of flavor)
- $^1/_2$ cup milk
- 1 egg

TO PUT ON TOP (YOU CHOOSE):

- Butter
- Real maple syrup
- Berries
- Sliced bananas
- Extra yogurt
- Powdered sugar

YIELD: This recipe makes about 5 pancakes.

TIME: It takes about 30 minutes to make and cook, start to finish.

YOU WILL ALSO NEED:

- Large wire-mesh strainer that fits over the bowl
- Medium-sized bowl
- Measuring cups and spoons
- Soup spoon
- Dinner knife for cutting butter
- Small bowl or pot for melting butter
- 2-cup liquid measure
- Small bowl for breaking the egg
- Whisk
- Wooden spoon
- Frying pan or griddle
- Metal spatula
- Plates and forks

ASK AN ADULT FOR HELP WITH:

- *Taking the melted butter out of the microwave or off the stove*
- *Checking to see if the pancakes are ready to flip and serve*

1

Put a strainer over a medium-sized bowl.
Put in the strainer:

1 cup **flour**

1/2 teaspoon **salt**

1 teaspoon **baking powder**

Gently shake the strainer up and down until everything sifts into the bowl.

With a soup spoon, make a dent in the center of the flour mixture. Put this aside for now.

2

Use a dinner knife to cut
1 tablespoon **butter.** Each line on
the butter wrapper means 1 tablespoon.

3

Put the butter in a small bowl and heat in the microwave on **high** for 30 seconds until it is melted. (Or melt it in a small pot on the stove over **low** heat.)

Ask an adult to take the butter out (or off the stove).

4

Spoon the **yogurt** into a 2-cup measuring cup until it reaches the line for 1 cup.

5

Pour 1/2 cup **milk** into the yogurt in the measuring cup (until together they reach the line for 1 1/2 cups).

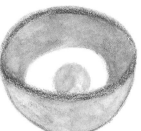

6

Break an **egg** into a small bowl.

Add this, plus the **melted butter,** to the yogurt and milk. Whisk until the egg disappears.

7

Pour the wet mixture into the dent in the dry mixture. Mix with a wooden spoon until you don't see any more flour.

8

Put a frying pan on the stove and turn on the heat to **medium.**

9

Use a dinner knife to cut a slice of butter.

Put it in the pan and push it around until it is melted all over the inside of the pan.

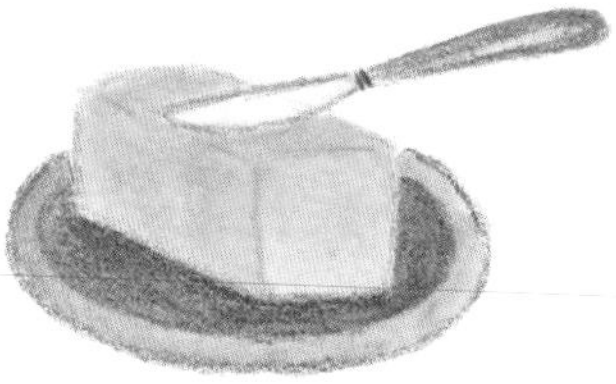

10

Scoop the batter with a $1/3$-cup measure and pour it into the pan to make as many round puddles as will fit.

11

Cook for 5 to 8 minutes on one side until golden brown underneath. (Use a spatula to peek and **ask an adult to help**.)

Flip the pancakes with a spatula and cook on the other side until golden brown underneath.

12

Serve hot—plain, or with **syrup, fruit**, extra yogurt, and/or **powdered sugar** on top.

TIME TO EAT!

Cinnamon Waffles

Popping frozen waffles into the toaster is easy and fun, and it turns an ordinary morning into a special occasion. Imagine just how much more special that morning might feel if the waffles are made fresh from real batter made by the real you!

This recipe has an unusual task in it. It involves beating egg whites (which actually are kind of yellowish) with an electric mixer until they become bright white and fluffy, like clouds. You will learn how to "separate" eggs, which means cracking the eggshell, opening up the eggs, and putting the yolks in one bowl and the whites in another. The other skill you will learn is how to "fold" the beaten egg whites into the batter, to puff it up. This makes the waffles so light they taste like crunchy cinnamon air.

If you don't eat all of the waffles, you can wrap the extra ones in a plastic bag and freeze them. Then just toast them in a toaster some other time, and they'll still be homemade.

TO "SEPARATE" THE EGGS BEFORE YOU BEGIN:

This is a job for two people. You will need 3 eggs, a funnel, a teaspoon, 2 small bowls, and a large bowl. One person holds the funnel over one of the small bowls. The other person cracks an egg hard on the edge of the bowl, right near the funnel. Using both thumbs, gently open the shell and immediately pour the insides of the egg into the funnel. The egg whites will slide down the funnel into the bowl. The yolk will stay in the funnel. Use the teaspoon to gently lift the yolk from the funnel, to let all of the egg white slip down, then slide the yolk into the other small bowl. If the egg white in the bowl has no yolk in it, transfer it to the large bowl. (It's okay if some whites get into the yolks, but it is very important that no yolks get into the whites! If you make mistakes, just save the mess-ups in a covered container in the refrigerator and use them some other time to make scrambled eggs.)

Continue this process with the remaining 2 eggs until you have a big bowl of just whites and a small bowl of just yolks.

NOTE TO THE ADULT:

This recipe calls for whole wheat pastry flour, which is available in most natural foods stores and in many grocery stores. If you can't find it, you can use all unbleached white flour.

INGREDIENTS:

- 3 eggs, separated (see above)
- 2 tablespoons sugar
- 1 cup unbleached white flour
- 3/4 cup whole wheat pastry flour
- 2 teaspoons baking powder
- 1/2 teaspoon baking soda
- 1/4 teaspoon salt
- 2 teaspoons cinnamon
- 3 tablespoons butter
- 1 1/2 cups milk
- 1 teaspoon vinegar (any kind)
- Can of vegetable oil cooking spray

TO PUT ON TOP OR ON THE SIDE (YOU CHOOSE):

- Real maple syrup
- Yogurt (any kind)
- Fruit salad
- Powdered sugar
- Extra butter

YIELD: This recipe makes 6 or 7 waffles.

TIME: It takes about 45 minutes to make and cook, start to finish.

YOU WILL ALSO NEED:

- Funnel with a 1/4-inch-diameter spout, and a teaspoon, for separating the eggs
- Large bowl for the egg whites
- 2 small bowls for the egg yolks
- Handheld electric mixer
- Large wire-mesh strainer that fits over the mixing bowl
- Large mixing bowl
- Measuring cups and spoons
- Dinner knife for cutting butter
- Small bowl or pot for melting butter
- 2-cup liquid measure
- Whisk
- Rubber spatula
- Waffle iron
- Plates and forks

ASK AN ADULT FOR HELP WITH:

- *Separating the eggs*
- *Using the electric mixer*
- *Taking the melted butter out of the microwave or off the stove*
- *Heating the waffle iron*
- *Closing the waffle iron (It can give out a blast of heat!)*

1

You have already separated the **eggs**. You have the **yolks** in one bowl and the **whites** in another, larger one. Right?

2

Add 1 tablespoon of the **sugar** to the egg whites.

3

Ask an adult to help with this step.

Beat the egg whites and sugar with an electric mixer on **high** speed until it looks like you have a bowl full of clouds.

Put this aside for now.

4

Put a strainer over a large mixing bowl. Put into the strainer:

1 cup **white flour**

3/4 cup **whole wheat pastry flour**

1 tablespoon sugar

2 teaspoons **baking powder**

1/2 teaspoon **baking soda**

1/4 teaspoon **salt**

2 teaspoons **cinnamon**

Gently shake the strainer up and down until everything sifts into the bowl. Put this aside for now.

5

Use a dinner knife to cut 3 tablespoons **butter.** Each line on the butter wrapper means 1 tablespoon.

6

Put the butter in a small bowl and heat it in the microwave on **high** for 1 minute until it is melted. (Or melt it in a small pot on the stove over **low** heat.)

Ask an adult to take the butter out (or off the stove).

7

Pour the **milk** into a 2-cup measuring cup until it reaches the line for 1 1/2 cups.

8

Add to the milk in the cup:
- 1 teaspoon **vinegar**
- the **melted butter**
- the egg yolks

Mix with a whisk until it is all one color.

9

Pour the **milk mixture** into the **flour mixture**. Stir with a wooden spoon until you don't see any more flour.

9 1/2

Pour the fluffy egg whites onto the batter. They will float on top.

10

"Fold" the "clouds" into the batter by lifting batter from the bottom with a rubber spatula and flopping it, little by little, on top. Do this about 10 times. There will be little fluffy bumps, and that's okay.

11

Spray the insides—top and bottom—of the waffle iron with **oil spray**.

Ask an adult to heat the waffle iron.

12

Scoop the batter with a 1/2-cup measure and put it in the center of the hot waffle iron in one blob. Don't spread it—just close the top.

Ask an adult to help.

13

Wait for about 4 minutes and then lift the top to see if the waffle is crunchy and brown. (It might need 1 or 2 minutes longer.)

Have a plate ready. Use a fork to lift the waffle onto the plate.

14

Serve hot— plain, or with **syrup, yogurt, fruit salad, powdered sugar,** or extra butter.

TIME TO EAT!

11

It's fun to make scrambled eggs, and it's easy to become a real pro.

Here's how you do it: First, beat the raw eggs in a bowl until they get all yellow and smooth. Next, melt some butter in a frying pan. (The butter keeps the eggs from sticking and gives them more flavor.) When you add the eggs and push them around in the pan, the heat turns them from a liquid into a soft solid. Take them out of the pan and eat them right away. Scrambled eggs taste best when they're hot and freshly cooked.

You might want a more experienced person standing by the first few times you try this, just for moral support. Once you get the hang of making scrambled eggs, you can make some toast to go with them. Put the bread in the toaster before you start cooking the eggs, so everything will be ready at approximately the same time. Congratulations! You are now a short-order breakfast chef!

INGREDIENTS:

- **2 eggs**
- **Salt in a shaker**
- **Butter for the pan**

EXTRAS (YOU CHOOSE):

- **Black pepper in a shaker**
- **2 teaspoons pesto (homemade or store-bought)**
- **1/4 cup grated cheese (any kind)**

YIELD: This recipe makes 1 serving.

TIME: It takes less than 5 minutes to make, start to finish.

YOU WILL ALSO NEED:

- Frying pan
- Small bowl for the eggs
- Fork for beating the eggs
- Spoon for adding pesto, if using
- Grater and plate for the cheese, if using
- Dinner knife for cutting the butter
- Fork or spatula for pushing the eggs in the pan
- Plate and fork

Should you ask an adult for help?

That's up to you, but make sure there is an adult in the house who knows you are doing this and can help you set up. (And, of course, if there is any task you feel uncomfortable doing, ask for help.)

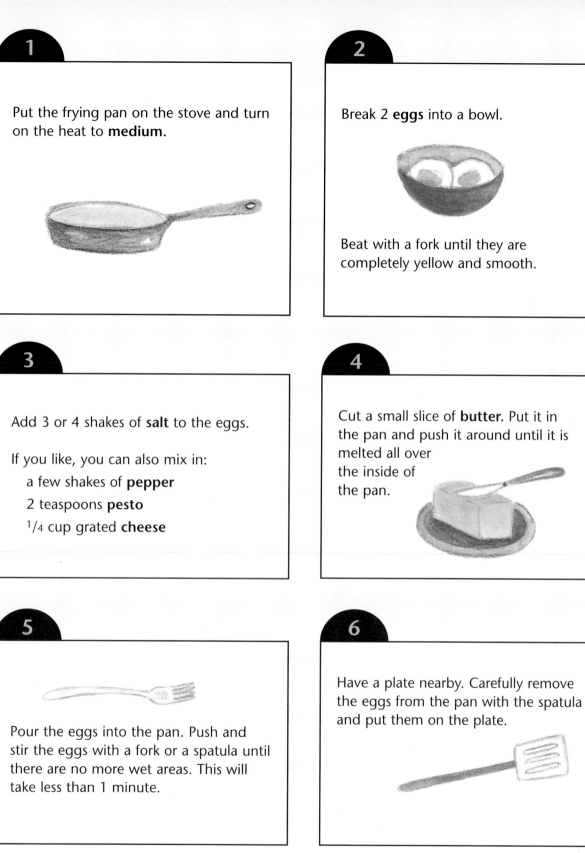

1

Put the frying pan on the stove and turn on the heat to **medium.**

2

Break 2 **eggs** into a bowl.

Beat with a fork until they are completely yellow and smooth.

3

Add 3 or 4 shakes of **salt** to the eggs.

If you like, you can also mix in:
    a few shakes of **pepper**
    2 teaspoons **pesto**
    1/4 cup grated **cheese**

4

Cut a small slice of **butter.** Put it in the pan and push it around until it is melted all over the inside of the pan.

5

Pour the eggs into the pan. Push and stir the eggs with a fork or a spatula until there are no more wet areas. This will take less than 1 minute.

6

Have a plate nearby. Carefully remove the eggs from the pan with the spatula and put them on the plate.

TIME TO EAT!

CORN MUFFINS

Some weekend soon, ask your parents if it's okay to get up early and make corn muffins for the family. It's pretty easy to do, and you will be the most popular person in the household!

Corn muffins taste best about 15 minutes after they've been baked, especially when you cut them open and spread them with butter so it melts right into them. But the muffins also toast well later on. If you have extras, keep them in the freezer in sealed plastic bags. Then you can defrost, slice, and toast them on school mornings.

Cornmeal is powdery, like flour, but it's kind of crunchy because it's made from ground dried corn. Its yellow color is the true yellow of the corn, and the corn also gives the muffins a slight crunch. We add regular flour to the batter, because regular flour is smooth and has something in it called "gluten" which holds the muffins together. The yogurt in the batter makes the muffins a little bit sour, so you may want to spread the muffins with jam or dip them in some maple syrup to sweeten them up. It's fun to pay attention to sweet and sour tastes when they hit your mouth at the same time!

INGREDIENTS:

- Can of vegetable oil cooking spray or canola oil
- 3 tablespoons butter
- 1 cup plain yogurt
- 1 large egg
- 1 cup cornmeal
- $1/4$ cup brown sugar
- 1 tablespoon white sugar
- 1 cup unbleached white flour
- 2 teaspoons baking powder
- $1/2$ teaspoon baking soda
- $1/2$ teaspoon salt

TO PUT ON TOP (YOU CHOOSE):

- Extra butter
- Your favorite jam
- Real maple syrup

YIELD: This recipe makes 6 muffins.

TIME: It takes about 15 minutes to make and another 20 minutes to bake. That's 35 minutes, start to finish.

"I've never done this before but I really like doing it!" —Karina

YOU WILL ALSO NEED:

- Brush for painting the pan with the oil, if using
- Dinner knife for cutting butter
- Small bowl or pot for melting butter
- 2-cup liquid measure
- Small bowl for breaking the egg
- Whisk
- Measuring spoons and cups
- Medium-sized mixing bowl
- Large wire-mesh strainer that fits over the mixing bowl
- Wooden spoon
- Rubber spatula
- Soup spoon for spooning batter into muffin cups
- Muffin pan with 6 standard-sized cups
- Timer with a bell
- Plate

ASK AN ADULT FOR HELP WITH:

- *Turning on the oven*
- *Taking the melted butter out of the microwave or off the stove*
- *Spooning the batter into the muffin cups*
- *Putting the muffins into the oven and taking them out*

1

Ask an adult to turn on the oven to 375°F.

2

Lightly spray the muffin cups with **oil spray** or paint them with a little **oil**.

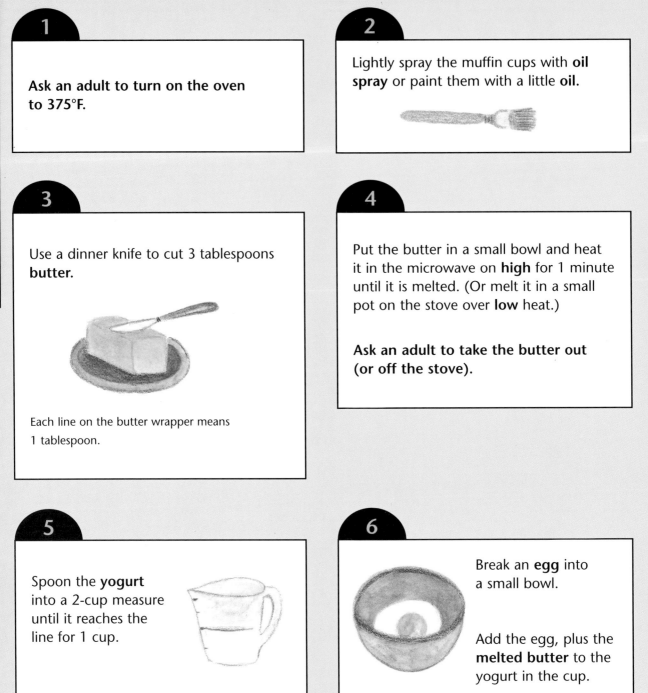

3

Use a dinner knife to cut 3 tablespoons **butter**.

Each line on the butter wrapper means 1 tablespoon.

4

Put the butter in a small bowl and heat it in the microwave on **high** for 1 minute until it is melted. (Or melt it in a small pot on the stove over **low** heat.)

Ask an adult to take the butter out (or off the stove).

5

Spoon the **yogurt** into a 2-cup measure until it reaches the line for 1 cup.

6

Break an **egg** into a small bowl.

Add the egg, plus the **melted butter** to the yogurt in the cup.

7

Whisk until it is all one color.

Put this aside for now.

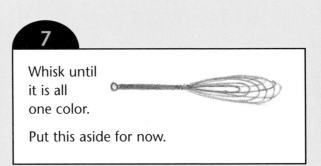

8

Measure 1 cup **cornmeal** and put it in a medium mixing bowl.

9

Measure 1/4 cup **brown sugar** plus 1 tablespoon **white sugar**.

Use your clean fingers to crumble the sugar into the cornmeal.

10

Place a strainer across the top of the bowl with the sugar. Put into the strainer:

- 1 cup **flour**
- 2 teaspoons **baking powder**
- 1/2 teaspoon **baking soda**
- 1/2 teaspoon **salt**

11

Gently shake the strainer up and down until everything sifts into the bowl. Take your time!

Mix with a wooden spoon until it is all one color. Make a dent in the center of the flour mixture with a spoon.

12

Scrape the **yogurt mixture** into the **flour mixture** with a rubber spatula.

Mix carefully with a wooden spoon until everything is wet and blended.

13

Use a soup spoon to carefully spoon the batter into the muffin cups.

Ask an adult for help—this is a little messy.

14

Ask an adult to put the pan in the oven.
Set the timer for 20 minutes.

Ask an adult to take the pan out of the oven and the muffins out of the pan.
Cool on a plate for 15 minutes.

TIME TO EAT!

If you've ever made popovers, this recipe will probably look familiar. It's almost the same batter, only this one has vanilla and some sugar added to make it taste more like a puffy pancake. Also, instead of making individual puffs, like popovers, you bake this batter in one big pan and then cut into squares. Use a large bowl for this so you can have fun and really let loose with the mixing without worrying about the batter flying out of the bowl and landing on the ceiling.

While the puff is in the oven, you can set the table with all of the different topping choices so everything is ready when it comes out.

Q: What makes it so puffy?

A: Four beaten eggs. They puff up from the heat of the oven.

INGREDIENTS:

- **1 tablespoon butter**
- **4 eggs**
- **1^1/$_3$ cups milk**
- **1 teaspoon vanilla extract**
- **3 tablespoons sugar**
- **1^1/$_2$ cups unbleached white flour**
- **^{1}/$_2$ teaspoon salt**

TO PUT ON TOP (YOU CHOOSE):

- **Yogurt (any kind)**
- **Real maple syrup**
- **Raspberries, blueberries, or blackberries**
- **Sliced bananas and/or strawberries**
- **Powdered sugar**

YIELD: This recipe makes 4 to 6 servings.

TIME: It takes about 10 minutes to make and another 35 minutes to bake. That's a total of 45 minutes, start to finish.

YOU WILL ALSO NEED:

- Dinner knife for cutting butter
- Small bowl or pot for melting butter
- 9 by 13-inch baking pan
- Rubber spatula
- Brush for spreading butter
- Large mixing bowl
- 2-cup liquid measure
- Measuring cups and spoons
- Whisk
- Timer with a bell
- Plates and forks

ASK AN ADULT FOR HELP WITH:

- *Turning on the oven*
- *Taking melted butter out of the microwave or off the stove*
- *Putting the pan into the oven and taking it out when the puff is done*

"When you are holding the bowl, don't hug it too, too close." —Rachel

1

Before you begin, **ask an adult to turn on the oven to 375°F.**

2

Use a dinner knife to cut 1 tablespoon **butter.** Each line on the butter wrapper means 1 tablespoon.

3

Put the butter in a small bowl and heat it in the microwave for 30 seconds on **high** until it is melted. (Or melt it in a small pot on the stove over **low** heat.)

Ask an adult to take it out (or off the stove).

4

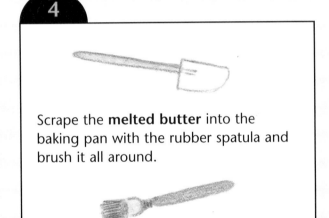

Scrape the **melted butter** into the baking pan with the rubber spatula and brush it all around.

5

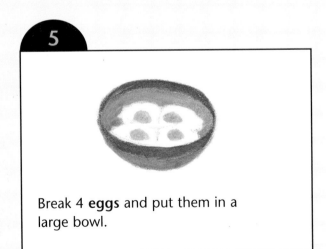

Break 4 **eggs** and put them in a large bowl.

6

Pour the **milk** into a 2-cup measure until it reaches the line for 1^1/$_3$ cups.

Pour this into the eggs.

7

Measure:

  1 teaspoon **vanilla extract**

  3 tablespoons **sugar**

Put these into the eggs and milk.

8

Whisk until it is all one color and smooth.

9

Measure:

  1 1/2 cups **flour**

  1/2 teaspoon **salt**

Put these into the wet mixture.

10

Whisk until you don't see any more flour and the lumps are gone. Scrape the sides of the bowl and mix it all in.

11

A two-person job:

  • One person holds the bowl and tilts it toward the pan.

  • The other person scrapes out all the batter with a rubber spatula.

12

Ask an adult to put the pan in the oven.

Set the timer for 35 minutes.

Ask an adult to take it out of the oven.

13

Cut the puff into squares and serve hot or warm, with **yogurt, maple syrup, berries, bananas,** and/or **powdered sugar** on top.

TIME TO EAT!

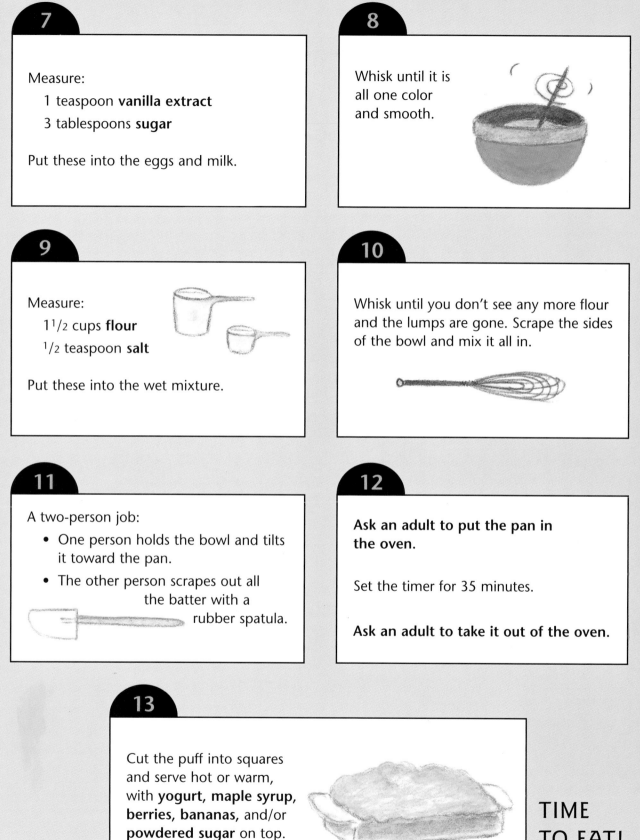

SMART COOKIES

("Eat 'em on the bus.")

These are like having your own homemade granola bars except they come out in squares instead of rectangles. Your parents probably don't want you eating cookies for breakfast on a regular basis, but once in a while, when you are late and don't have time to sit down and eat, they might let you grab a few of these as you're running out the door. There is some real nutrition in these cookies: lots of rolled oats (which is what oatmeal is made from) and oat bran or wheat germ—plus apple juice and applesauce. (And you can also choose to add nuts and/or dried fruit.) You can be very creative with this easy recipe!

In addition to being a breakfast food, Smart Cookies make very good snacks. They are healthier for you than most cookies, and they also give you extra energy. They travel well, and freeze well in sealed plastic bags, so one batch can last you a while.

You will notice an unusual step in this recipe. After the cookies are baked in the pan, they are cut, moved to a tray, and then baked some more. Why? Because this allows the heat to toast them in more places, so they can become crunchy all over.

INGREDIENTS:

- Can of vegetable oil cooking spray or a little canola oil
- 1 1/2 cups unbleached white flour (or 3/4 cup each of unbleached white flour and whole wheat pastry flour)
- 2 cups rolled oats
- 1/4 cup oat bran or wheat germ
- 1/2 teaspoon cinnamon
- 1/2 teaspoon salt
- 2/3 cup brown sugar
- 1 cup apple juice
- 1/2 cup unsweetened applesauce
- 1/4 cup canola oil
- 1 teaspoon vanilla extract
- 3/4 cup semisweet chocolate chips

EXTRAS (YOU CHOOSE):

- 1/2 cup dried cranberries or dried cherries
- 1/2 cup shredded unsweetened coconut
- 1/2 cup chopped peanuts or almonds

YIELD: This recipe makes about 24 squares.

TIME: It takes about 10 minutes to make, 45 minutes to bake, and 15 minutes to cool down. That's about an hour and 10 minutes, start to finish.

YOU WILL ALSO NEED:

- Brush for painting the pan with oil, if using
- 9 by 13-inch baking pan
- Large mixing bowl
- Measuring cups and spoons
- Wooden spoon
- Sharp knife to cut the cookies
- Spatula
- Baking tray
- Timer with a bell

ASK AN ADULT FOR HELP WITH:

- *Turning on the oven*
- *Putting the pan into the oven and taking it out*
- *Cutting the baked cookies into squares and putting them on the tray*
- *Putting the tray into the oven and taking it out*

1

Before you start, **ask an adult to turn on the oven to 375°F.**

Spray or brush the pan with **oil.**

2

Put in a large bowl:

- 1 1/2 cups **flour**
- 2 cups **oats**
- 1/4 cup **oat bran** or **wheat germ**
- 1/2 teaspoon **cinnamon**
- 1/2 teaspoon **salt**

3

Add 2/3 cup **brown sugar.** Mix it in with your very clean fingers. Make a dent with a wooden spoon in the center of the mixture.

4

Pour in:

- 1 cup **apple juice**
- 1/2 cup **applesauce**
- 1/4 cup oil
- 1 teaspoon **vanilla extract**
- 3/4 cup **chocolate chips**

5

If you like, you can also add all or some of these:

- 1/2 cup **dried cranberries** or **dried cherries**
- 1/2 cup **coconut**
- 1/2 cup chopped **peanuts** or **almonds**

6

Mix slowly with a wooden spoon— or with your hands— until everything is damp and you don't see any more flour.

7

Scoop out all of the batter from the bowl and spread and pat it evenly in the pan.

8

Ask an adult to put the pan in the oven. Set the timer for 30 minutes.

Ask an adult to take the pan out of the oven and cut the rectangle into squares.

Put the squares on a baking tray.

8 1/2

Ask an adult to put the tray in the oven. Bake for 15 minutes longer.

Ask an adult to remove the pan from the oven. Cool for 15 minutes before serving.

TIME TO EAT!

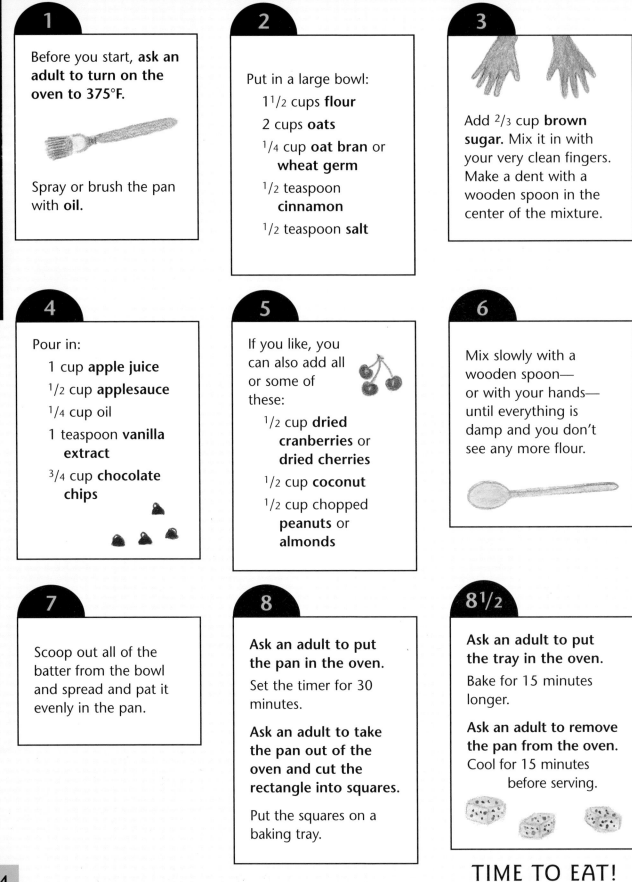

Best Hot Cocoa with Real Whipped Cream

There is a secret ingredient in this recipe for deep, chocolatey cocoa: chocolate chips! You melt them right into the milk in a pot on the stove. It tastes heavenly!

INGREDIENTS:

- 2 tablespoons semisweet chocolate chips
- $1/2$ teaspoon sugar
- $1 1/2$ cups milk (lowfat is okay)
- A pinch of salt
- $1/8$ teaspoon vanilla extract

TO PUT ON TOP (YOU CHOOSE):

- Whipped cream (recipe follows)
- Cinnamon

YIELD: This recipe makes 1 large or 2 small servings.

TIME: It takes about 10 minutes to make, start to finish.

YOU WILL ALSO NEED:

- Measuring spoons
- Small saucepan
- 2-cup liquid measure
- Wooden spoon
- 1 or 2 mugs

ASK AN ADULT FOR HELP WITH:

- *Deciding when the cocoa is hot enough*
- *Pouring the cocoa*

REAL WHIPPED CREAM

For a special treat, you can make some whipped cream to put on top. It's really fun to do this by hand, with a friend to help.

- 1 cup whipping cream
- $1/2$ teaspoon vanilla extract
- 3 tablespoons powdered sugar

Get out a large bowl and a whisk. Put the cream, vanilla, and powdered sugar in the bowl. Beat strongly but not too fast with the whisk. It's best to take turns with someone, so your arm won't get tired. When it gets nice and puffy but is still soft, it's ready.

YIELD: This makes more than enough whipped cream for 1 or 2 mugs of the Best Hot Cocoa.

TIME: It takes 5 to 10 minutes to make, start to finish. Store the extra in a covered container in the refrigerator for up to 1 or 2 days.

1

Put 2 tablespoons **chocolate chips** plus $^1/_2$ teaspoon **sugar** into a small saucepan.

2

Pour the **milk** into a 2-cup measuring cup until it reaches the line for $1^1/_2$ cups.

3

Slowly pour the milk into the saucepan.

Add:

a pinch of **salt**

$^1/_8$ teaspoon **vanilla extract**

4

Put the pan on the stove and turn on the heat to **medium.**

5

Stir *slowly* with a wooden spoon as the milk heats up. The chocolate chips will slowly melt.

It takes about 5 minutes to reach the perfect temperature. Keep stirring and be patient. Do not let it boil.

6

How can you tell when it's ready?

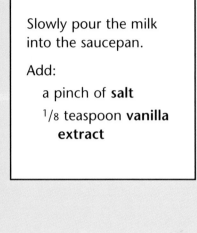

Ask an adult to help decide.

7

When it's hot, take the cocoa off the stove and slowly pour it from the pot into 1 or 2 mugs.

You might want an adult to help.

8

Serve plain, or with a little **whipped cream** and/or **cinnamon** on top.

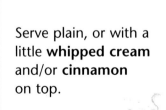

TIME TO DRINK!

CHAPTER 2

SOUPS, SANDWICHES, AND SALADS FOR LUNCH OR DINNER

Eggflower Soup

Eggs are not plants, as I'm sure you know, and therefore they don't grow flowers. So what's up with the name of this soup?

I'll tell you. When beaten eggs are poured slowly into a pot of steaming-hot broth, they cook themselves—boom!—right on contact. It's sort of like eggs that scramble themselves. Where does the flower part come in? When eggs cook so suddenly, they puff up, or "blossom," like a flower opening up. And "Eggflower Soup" is a much nicer name than "Scrambled Egg Soup."

Soup with an egg in it is traditional in several cultures: Chinese, Italian, and Greek are just a few. Our version has Chinese flavors—soy sauce, scallion, and sesame oil (which has the most wonderful smell). This soup also has little cubes of tofu, which look like miniature dice and are fun to eat.

The flavor of the broth is very important, so use a kind that tastes good to you. Ask your parents to buy several different kinds of vegetable broth for you to taste, so you can discover a brand you really like. I usually find my own favorite brand of vegetable broth (called "Imagine") in the natural foods section of the grocery store. It's the kind that comes packed in a rectangular 1-quart "box" with a spout on top.

"My advice is to use a fat carrot for this, so you won't grate your hand."
—Sophia

INGREDIENTS:

- 1 quart (4 cups) vegetable broth
- 1 medium-sized carrot, peeled
- 4 scallions
- $1/2$ pound firm tofu
- 2 eggs
- A few drops of sesame oil (as much as tastes good to you)
- A few drops of soy sauce (as much as tastes good to you)

YIELD: This recipe makes 4 to 6 servings.

TIME: It takes 15 minutes to make, start to finish.

YOU WILL ALSO NEED:

- Liquid measuring cup
- Soup pot
- Peeler, grater, and small bowl for the carrot
- Small bowl for the carrot, cut scallions, and tofu
- Small, sharp knife for cutting scallions and tofu
- Cutting board
- Small bowl for the eggs
- Fork for beating the eggs
- Wooden spoon
- Ladle, bowls, and spoons

Should you ask an adult for help?

That's up to you, but make sure there is an adult in the house who knows you are doing this and can help you set up. (And, of course, if there is any task you feel uncomfortable doing, ask for help.)

1

Measure 4 cups **broth** and pour it into a soup pot. Put the pot on the stove and turn on the heat to **medium.**

2

Meanwhile, grate a **carrot.** Put it in a bowl.

3

Trim the "hairy" tip from 4 **scallions,** and then cut them into tiny pieces on the cutting board.

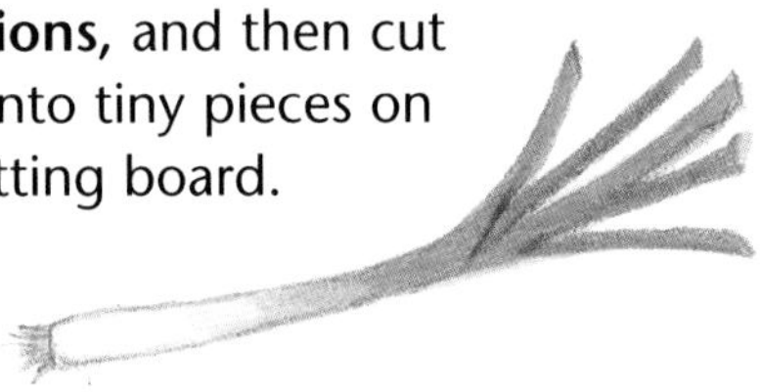

Include the whole white part and the lower half of the green part. Put them in the bowl with the carrots.

4

Cut 2 chunks of **tofu** into little cubes, like dice. Add them to the bowl of vegetables.

5

Break 2 **eggs** into a small bowl.

6

Beat the eggs with a fork until they are all yellow and smooth.

7

Use the wooden spoon to carefully push the carrots, scallions, and tofu into the broth.

8

Turn up the heat to **high** and wait for the broth to boil.

You can listen to some music while you are waiting.

9

When the soup boils, pour in the beaten eggs and stir.

The eggs will puff up right in the soup!

10

Ladle the soup into bowls.

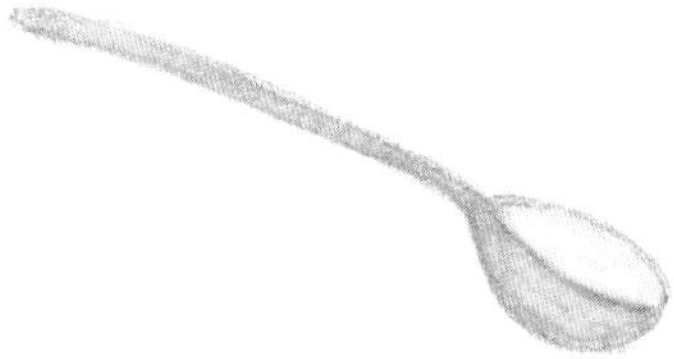

11

Add a few drops *each* of **soy sauce** and **sesame oil** to your bowl of soup.

TIME TO EAT!

CREAMY CORN SOUP

Have you ever heard the expression "comfort food"? It usually means food that is warm and smooth, with a mild flavor that makes you feel relaxed and cozy. Creamy soups are definitely comfort food. Here is one you can make quite easily for lunch, dinner, or a warm snack on a rainy day.

A creamy soup doesn't always actually contain cream, which is very rich and fatty. Sometimes the creaminess just comes from whipping the vegetables and broth together in a blender or food processor until they make a smooth, thick liquid, called a "purée" (pronounced "pure-ay"). That is how you make this delicious, creamy corn soup. But there is some milk in this recipe. If you like, you can use lowfat milk to make a lighter soup. Because of the puréed corn, it will still taste rich.

You can use canned, frozen, or fresh corn for this recipe. If you're using frozen corn, just put it in a strainer first and run some water over it—directly from the faucet—for about 2 minutes. That will defrost it enough. If you are using fresh corn, **ask an adult to scrape it off the cob with a small, sharp knife.** (You will need about 3 ears of corn.)

If you're using canned corn and it is packed in just water and salt with no sugar, the liquid from the can might taste good enough to use in the soup. Taste it, and if you like it, go ahead and use it instead of broth. Otherwise, use vegetable broth. There are some very good varieties available in the supermarket these days. (See what it says about broth on page 28.)

"Let's get it really smooth." —Izzi

"It *is* really smooth!" —Karina

"So what? Let's get it smoother." —Izzi

INGREDIENTS:

- 1 tablespoon butter
- 6 scallions, minced (trim the "hairy" tip, and cut the white and lower half of green part in tiny pieces)
- 1 stalk celery, chopped small
- 2 cups corn
- $1/2$ teaspoon salt
- $1/2$ teaspoon dried basil
- 1 cup vegetable broth or the strained liquid from the can of corn
- 1 cup milk

YIELD: This recipe makes 4 to 6 servings.

TIME: It takes about 40 minutes to make, start to finish.

YOU WILL ALSO NEED:

- Small, sharp knife and a cutting board for cutting the vegetables ahead of time
- Can opener, wire-mesh strainer, plus a bowl the strainer fits over, if you are using canned corn
- Medium-sized saucepan with a lid
- Dinner knife for cutting butter
- Wooden spoon
- 1-cup liquid measure
- Blender or food processor fitted with the steel blade
- Ladle, bowls, and spoons

ASK AN ADULT FOR HELP WITH:

- *Uncovering the pot and deciding when the liquid is hot enough*
- *Setting up the blender or food processor and transferring the soup to it*
- *Taking the puréed soup out of the blender or food processor*

1

Put a medium-sized saucepan on the stove and turn on the heat to **low.**

2

Use a dinner knife to cut 1 tablespoon **butter.** Each line on the butter wrapper means 1 tablespoon.

3

Put the butter into the saucepan and push it around until it melts.

4

Add:
- the **scallions**
- the **celery**
- the **corn**
- 1/2 teaspoon **salt**
- 1/2 teaspoon **basil**

5

Turn the heat up to **medium.**

Stir and cook the vegetables for about 8 minutes.

6

Add 1 cup **broth** or **corn liquid** and turn up the heat until it begins to boil.

Ask an adult to help decide when it's hot enough.

7

Turn the heat down to **low** and cover the pot.

8

Let it cook with the cover on for 5 minutes.

9

Meanwhile, measure 1 cup **milk**.

10

Ask an adult to help with this step.

Uncover the soup and carefully pour it into a blender or a food processor. Pour in the milk, and purée until it is smooth.

11

Ask an adult to help here, too.

Pour the puréed soup back into the same saucepan. Heat it just a little if it has cooled down, then ladle it into bowls, and serve.

TIME TO EAT!

TOMATO SOUP

WITH CRISPY CROUTONS

Making homemade soup can be a lot simpler than it may seem. The broth for this tomato soup is made from tomatoes that are puréed (blended smooth in a blender) in their own juice. The onions and garlic give the soup flavor, and the very special croutons that you make yourself give it a fun, crunchy topping.

You might find that you like the croutons so much, you want to make them all by themselves sometime to eat as a snack or to put on salads. You can use any kind of bread. Different breads make different-tasting croutons—and they all taste great!

INGREDIENTS:

- $1/3$ cup plus 2 tablespoons olive oil
- 3 teaspoons minced garlic (cut in tiny pieces)
- 6 to 8 slices French, Italian, or sourdough bread
- 1 cup minced onion (cut in tiny pieces)
- $1/2$ teaspoon salt
- 1 (28-ounce) can whole, peeled tomatoes, with liquid
- 1 cup milk

EXTRAS (YOU CHOOSE):

- A sprig of fresh dill
- A few fresh basil leaves

"The soup looks kind of weird, but it tastes actually very good." —Jesse

36

YIELD: This recipe makes 4 or 5 servings, with extra croutons.

TIME: It takes about 1 hour to prepare, start to finish, including the crouton-making time.

YOU WILL ALSO NEED:

- Small, sharp knife and a cutting board for cutting the vegetables ahead of time
- 1-cup liquid measure
- Small bowl for the olive oil
- Measuring spoons and cups
- Brush for painting the bread with oil
- Cutting board
- Dinner knife or bread knife for cutting bread
- Baking tray
- Medium-sized saucepan
- Wooden spoon
- Can opener
- Blender or food processor fitted with the steel blade
- Ladle, bowls, and spoons
- Scissors, if you're adding the dill or basil

ASK AN ADULT FOR HELP WITH:

- *Turning on the oven*
- *Putting the tray into the oven*
- *Deciding when the croutons are ready and taking the tray out of the oven*
- *Opening the can of tomatoes*
- *Setting up the blender or food processor and transferring the puréed tomatoes to the saucepan*
- *Deciding when the soup is hot*

37

1

Ask an adult to turn on the oven to 375°F.

2

Measure $1/3$ cup **olive oil** and pour it into a bowl.

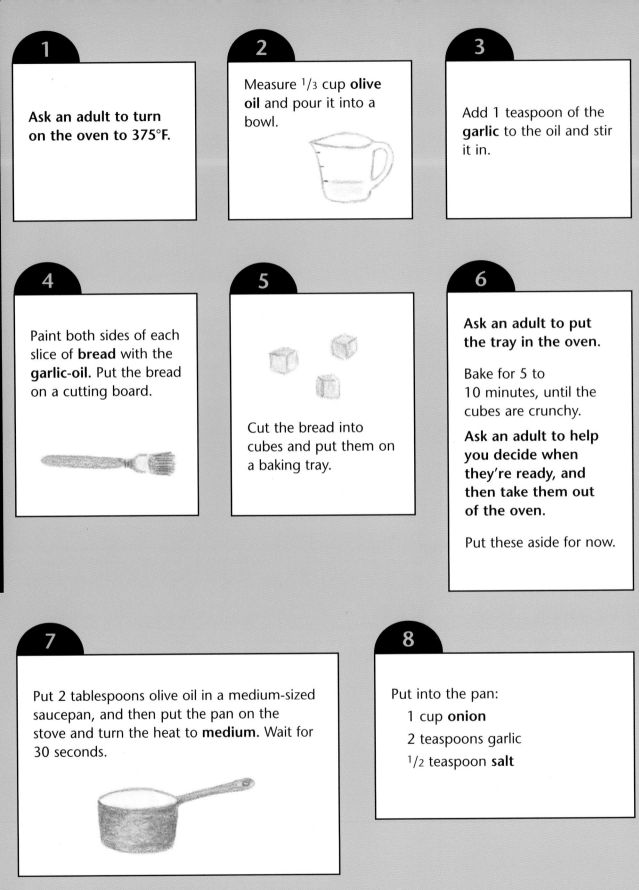

3

Add 1 teaspoon of the **garlic** to the oil and stir it in.

4

Paint both sides of each slice of **bread** with the **garlic-oil.** Put the bread on a cutting board.

5

Cut the bread into cubes and put them on a baking tray.

6

Ask an adult to put the tray in the oven.

Bake for 5 to 10 minutes, until the cubes are crunchy.

Ask an adult to help you decide when they're ready, and then take them out of the oven.

Put these aside for now.

7

Put 2 tablespoons olive oil in a medium-sized saucepan, and then put the pan on the stove and turn the heat to **medium.** Wait for 30 seconds.

8

Put into the pan:

1 cup **onion**

2 teaspoons garlic

$1/2$ teaspoon **salt**

9

Cook and stir the onions and garlic for 10 minutes.

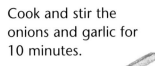

The onions will become soft, and it will smell really good.

10

Ask an adult to help you open the can of tomatoes.

Put the **tomatoes** and all of their liquid into a blender or a food processor. Add the cooked onions and garlic, and purée until smooth.

11

Ask an adult to help you with this step.

Pour the puréed mixture back into the saucepan.

12

Put the saucepan on the stove again and turn the heat to **medium.**

13

While the soup heats up, measure 1 cup **milk.**

14

Ask an adult to help you decide when the soup is hot.

When it is hot, slowly pour in the milk. Heat for just a few minutes, but don't let it boil.

15

Ladle the soup into serving bowls.

If you like, you can snip tiny bits of fresh **dill** or **basil** with scissors right over the bowls of soup.

16

Put the **croutons** in a separate bowl and pass them around at the table so people can take some and float them in their bowls of soup.

TIME TO EAT!

MACARONI MINESTRONE

This minestrone is so thick with vegetables, pasta, and beans, it's a really more of a stew than a soup. You can even serve it for lunch or dinner as a main dish, with a salad and some bread on the side. Everyone will be quite full and happy. Another nice thing to do with Macaroni Minestrone is to heat some up and pack it in a wide-mouth thermos to take to school with you for lunch. What a cozy treat! (Just don't forget to pack a spoon.)

This recipe is a nice one to make with a friend, because there's quite a bit of preparation needed before you start the cooking, and it's fun to share the tasks. You'll need to wash and chop celery and zucchini, to mince (cut in tiny pieces) an onion and some garlic, and to cut baby carrots into small pieces. After the vegetables are cut, put them into three separate small bowls, with the onions in one, the celery, carrots, and garlic together in another, and the zucchini by itself in the third.

When all of the ingredients are in place near the cooking area, the rest of the work will be easy. The hardest part will be waiting for the minestrone to cook! (You and your friend could do card tricks while you wait. Just be sure to stay by the pot so you'll be there when the soup needs you.)

INTERESTING FACT: This soup becomes thicker and more like a stew if it sits around for an hour or two after you make it. Why is that? Because the beans and the macaroni absorb some of the tomato juice.

"I love chopping with small, nice, sharp knives." —Noah

"It's good to cut the celery in little bunches of small strips." —Yaeir

INGREDIENTS:

- 2 tablespoons olive oil
- 1 cup minced onion (cut in tiny pieces)
- $1/2$ teaspoon salt
- 1 teaspoon dried basil
- $1/4$ teaspoon dried oregano
- $1/4$ teaspoon dried thyme
- 1 stalk celery, chopped
- 2 teaspoons minced (cut in tiny pieces) or crushed garlic
- 10 baby carrots, sliced
- 1 small zucchini, sliced
- 6 cups tomato juice (a 1-pound, 14-ounce bottle or can)
- 1 cup uncooked macaroni
- 1 (15-ounce) can chickpeas, navy beans, or kidney beans, rinsed and drained in a wire-mesh strainer or a colander over the sink
- Grated parmesan cheese for the top

YIELD: This recipe makes 5 or 6 servings.

TIME: It takes about 45 minutes to make, start to finish.

YOU WILL ALSO NEED:

- Small, sharp knife and a cutting board for cutting the vegetables ahead of time
- Garlic press, if crushing garlic
- Can opener
- Wire-mesh strainer or colander for the beans
- Soup pot with a lid
- Measuring cup and spoons
- Wooden spoon
- Ladle, bowls, and spoons

ASK AN ADULT FOR HELP WITH:

- *Setting up the vegetable chopping area*
- *Chopping the onion and possibly the other vegetables also*
- *Opening the cans of tomato juice and beans, and rinsing the beans*
- *Lifting the lid on the pot before each stirring (Hot steam will escape when the lid is lifted!)*
- *Adding macaroni to the pot and checking the macaroni to see if it's done*

1

Measure 2 tablespoons of **olive oil** into a soup pot.

2

Put the pot on the stove and turn on the heat to **medium**. Wait for about 30 seconds.

3

Slowly add the onions to the pot. Stir and then wait for about 2 minutes.

4

Sprinkle in:

$1/2$ teaspoon **salt**

1 teaspoon **basil**

$1/4$ teaspoon **oregano**

$1/4$ teaspoon **thyme**

5

Stir, and then wait for another 2 minutes.

6

Stir in:

the **celery**

the **garlic**

the **carrots**

Put on the lid and wait for 2 more minutes.

7

Add the **zucchini,** stir again, and wait for 1 minute.

8

Slowly pour in all the **tomato juice.** Turn up the heat to **high** and wait until it boils. This will take about 5 to 8 minutes.

9

Waiting for the soup to boil...

you could do card tricks.

10

You might need adult help with this step.

Slowly add the **macaroni.** Stir carefully from the bottom of the pot with a wooden spoon.

11

Cover the pot and turn down the heat to **medium.** Wait for 2 minutes.

12

Ask an adult to lift the lid.

Stir the soup from the bottom. Put the lid back on.

13

Wait for about 5 more minutes.

Ask an adult to help decide if the macaroni is done.

14

When the macaroni is done, gently stir in the **beans.**

15

Ladle the soup into bowls, sprinkle with **parmesan,** and serve.

TIME TO EAT!

Grilled Cheese & Broccoli Sandwich

If you already love broccoli, this sandwich might become your all-time favorite at-home lunch. If you are having trouble appreciating broccoli, this sandwich *still* might become your all-time favorite at-home lunch!

You see, broccoli tastes very good with cheese melted on it, especially if the broccoli is cooked with some onions beforehand. And even though onions might seem nasty when they are raw, they become very sweet and smell wonderful when they are cooked. So give this sandwich a try. And make it for others, too. It will become a favorite, I promise.

"I like how the vegetables are strapped down by the melted cheese." —Sam

Once you get comfortable with this recipe, you can experiment by substituting other vegetables. The cooking method will be exactly the same. Try using cauliflower, which also tastes terrific with cheese. You can break cauliflower into little pieces with your hands, and you won't need a knife at all. Zucchini is another vegetable that works very well in this sandwich. Have an adult help you cut it into little strips first, and then cut the strips crosswise to make tiny dice shapes.

INGREDIENTS:

- $1/3$ cup plus 2 tablespoons olive oil
- $1/2$ cup minced red onion (cut in tiny pieces)
- 2 cups chopped broccoli
- $1/2$ teaspoon salt
- $1/2$ teaspoon dried thyme
- 8 slices bread (sourdough, rye, or wheat)
- 2 cups grated cheddar cheese

YIELD: This recipe makes about 4 big servings.

TIME: It takes about 40 minutes, start to finish.

YOU WILL ALSO NEED:

- Small, sharp knife and a cutting board for preparing the vegetables ahead of time
- Handheld grater or food processor fitted with the grating attachment for grating the cheese ahead of time
- Measuring spoons
- Frying pan with a lid
- Wooden spoon
- 1-cup liquid measure
- Brush for painting oil onto the bread
- Spatula
- Soup spoon
- Plates

ASK AN ADULT FOR HELP WITH:

- *Cutting the onion and broccoli*
- *Setting up the food processor (if using) and taking the cheese out of it*
- *Deciding when the broccoli is cooked enough*
- *Transferring the cooked vegetables from the pan to the bowl*
- *Wiping out the frying pan*
- *Lifting the lid to see if the cheese has melted (Hot steam will escape when the lid is lifted!)*

1

Measure 2 tablespoons of the **olive oil** into a frying pan.

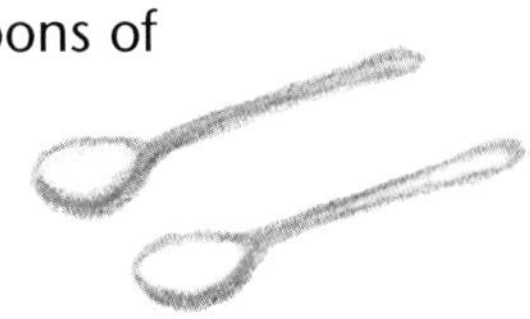

Put the pan on the stove and turn on the heat to **medium.**

Wait for 30 seconds and then add the **onions.**

2

Stir and cook the onions for about 2 minutes, then add the **broccoli.**

2 1/2

Sprinkle in:
  1/2 teaspoon **salt**
  1/2 teaspoon **dried thyme**

3

Stir and cook for about 8 minutes, or until the broccoli is bright green and just a little soft.

Ask an adult to help you decide when it's done.

4

This is a two-person job to do with an adult:

- The adult holds the pan and tilts it toward a bowl.

- You scrape all the vegetables into the bowl.

- The adult wipes out the frying pan with a paper towel so you can use it again.

5

Measure 1/3 cup olive oil.

6

Dip the brush in the oil and paint each slice of **bread** on both sides with the olive oil.

7

Put the frying pan back on the stove and turn on the heat to **medium**.

8

Put 1 or 2 slices of the **oiled bread** in the pan and cook until the bread is golden brown underneath. (Use a spatula to peek.) This will take a few minutes.

9

Flip the bread over and turn the heat down to **low**.

10

Use a soup spoon to put some of the broccoli mixture in the center of each piece of bread in the frying pan.

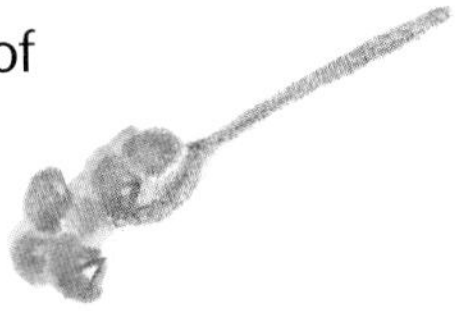

11

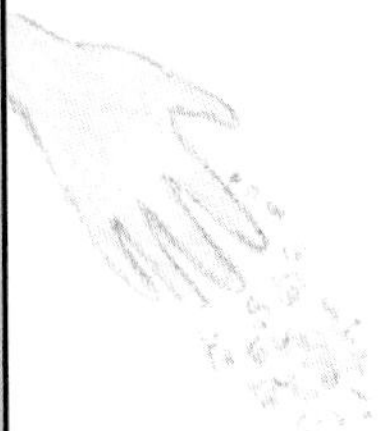

Sprinkle some **cheese** over the broccoli mixture. Cover the pan to help the cheese melt sooner. Wait for about 3 minutes.

12

Ask an adult to help with this:

Carefully lift the lid to see if the cheese has melted. Also, peek underneath the bread to see if the bottom has turned golden brown.

13

When the sandwich is ready, use a spatula to lift it out of the pan and put it on a plate. Wait a minute or two for the cheese to cool down a little.

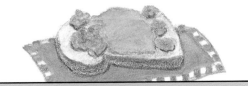

TIME TO EAT!

Pita Spirals

When is a sandwich not like a sandwich at all? How about when it's rolled up into a spiral and cut into pieces to show off the beautiful food design on the inside? This recipe is not difficult, it's just a little bit messy. Keep plenty of paper towels nearby.

NOTE: You can use flour tortillas instead of pita bread. (You won't have to snip them in half.)

INGREDIENTS:

- 1 pita bread (or 2 flour tortillas)
- 1/2 cup cream cheese, at room temperature
- 4 chives, 1 sprig of dill, and/or 3 basil leaves (optional)
- 1 medium-sized ripe tomato, sliced into thin rounds
- 6 large, crisp spinach leaves, washed and dried

YIELD: This recipe makes 2 or 3 servings.

TIME: It takes about 20 minutes, start to finish.

YOU WILL ALSO NEED:

- Scissors
- Cutting board
- Small bowl for the cream cheese
- Dinner knife for spreading the cream cheese
- Steak knife for cutting the tomato and the sandwich
- Paper towels to wipe messy hands
- Plates

Should you ask an adult for help?

That's up to you, but make sure there is an adult in the house who knows you are doing this and can help you set up. (And, of course, if there is any task you feel uncomfortable doing, ask for help.)

48

1

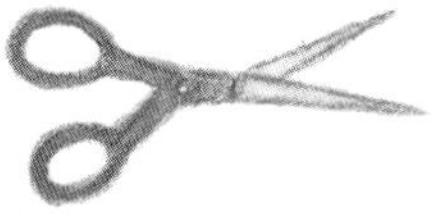

Snip around the edges of a **pita bread** with scissors to separate it into 2 halves. Put the circles down on the cutting board with the inside part facing up.

2

Put the soft **cream cheese** in a small bowl. Use a scissors to snip tiny pieces of **chives, dill,** and/or **basil** over the bowl, if you'd like to add them.

3

Spread a thin layer of cream cheese onto each pita circle.

4

Put 3 **tomato slices** in a row down the middle. They can be on top of each other a little.

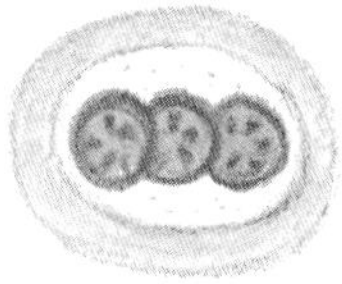

5

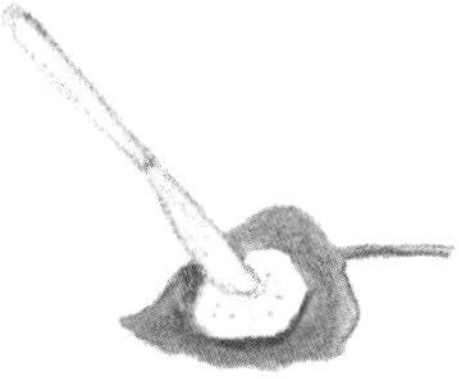

Spread some cream cheese onto 2 or 3 **spinach leaves.**

This might be a little messy. Take your time.

6

Lay the "frosted" spinach leaves on top of the tomatoes, with the cream cheese facing up.

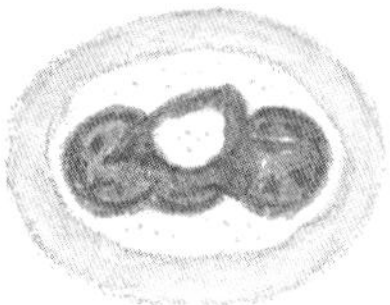

7

Roll up the circle, pressing the edges tightly closed. You will end up with a log shape.

8

Cut the log crosswise into 3 or 4 pieces to show the lovely spiral design inside.

TIME TO EAT!

BEAN DIP AND TORTILLA CHIP SANDWICH

Take out your favorite bean dip. (You can make your own—see page 152.) Spread it as thickly as you like on a slice of bread or toast and then press some tortilla chips into it until they stick. You can also add a little salsa. (There's a recipe for salsa on page 154, or use some store-bought.) Put another slice of bread or toast on top, cut in half, and eat.

You can also use a corn muffin instead of bread. (There's a recipe on page 14.) Cut the muffin in half, toast it if you like, and put a little bean dip on each half. Press in a few chips and put maybe just a drop of salsa on top. Eat it open-faced. It's quite wonderful!

CREAM CHEESE AND APRICOT SANDWICH

Spread some softened cream cheese on a bagel or a piece of banana bread (recipe on page 134). Take about 4 dried apricots— the soft kind, if you have them—and use scissors to cut them into little strips. Press the pieces of apricot onto the cream cheese, either randomly or in a pattern. That's it! Enjoy.

EGG SALAD AND CUCUMBER SANDWICH

Ask an adult to hard-boil and peel 2 eggs
(unless you feel comfortable doing these
things yourself and an adult in your home
says it's okay). Put the peeled eggs in a
shallow dish and mash them with a fork
until they are a pile of tiny pieces. Add
about 3 shakes of salt from a salt shaker
and 1 tablespoon mayonnaise. Mix until all
of the egg is damp with mayonnaise.

"I'm gonna eat a whole sandwich to decide
if I like it or not, because you can't really tell
if you only take a little bite."
—Zach

Using a vegetable peeler, peel a cucumber and slice it into thin pieces with a
small, sharp knife. **(You might need an
adult to help with this step.)** Spread some
egg salad on slices of bread or toast and
arrange a few cucumber slices on top.
You can put another slice of bread or toast
on top, or just eat it open-faced. This will
make enough egg salad for two or three
people, depending on whether it is for
lunch or a snack.

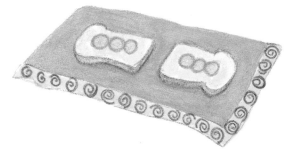

The World's Best Peanut Butter

Just like cornmeal is made from grinding up corn, peanut butter is made from grinding up peanuts. It's really fun to make your own.

Here's how it works: Peanuts are naturally filled with oil. When you buzz them for a while in a blender or food processor, they burst into pieces that get tinier and tinier the longer you run the machine. As they grind up like this, more and more of their oil comes out, making them softer and mushier until, finally, the little pieces are so soft and mushy, they're paste.

Now you can spread it! Try some of this peanut butter on bread with jam or jelly or other yummy things like honey and bananas. Sliced grapes, apples, or peaches are also good. And how about a peanut butter sandwich with raisins, dried cranberries, and toasted coconut? Really! Give it a try.

NOTE: You can make chunky-style peanut butter by blending for only 1 or 2 minutes. Peanut butter will keep for months in the refrigerator if stored in a tightly covered container.

INGREDIENTS:
- 1¹/₂ cups peanuts (raw or roasted)
- ¹/₄ teaspoon salt (if the peanuts are unsalted)
- 1 tablespoon plus 1 teaspoon peanut oil or canola oil

YIELD: This recipe makes about 1 cup.

TIME: It takes about 5 minutes to make, start to finish.

YOU WILL ALSO NEED:
- Measuring cups and spoons
- Blender or food processor fitted with the steel blade
- Dinner knife and/or a narrow rubber spatula for scraping the peanut butter out of the machine
- Jar or container with a lid

ASK AN ADULT FOR HELP WITH:
- *Setting up the blender or food processor and scraping down the sides, if necessary*
- *Taking the peanut butter out of the machine*
- *Cleaning the blades of the machine afterwards*

1

Measure 1 1/2 cups **peanuts.** Put them into a blender or food processor.

2

If the peanuts are unsalted, add 1/4 teaspoon **salt.**

If you don't know whether or not the peanuts are salted, taste them.

3

Turn on the machine. (Use the "chop" or "blend" speed if you're using a blender.)

The peanuts will begin crunching up. It will be loud at first.

4

Keep running the machine for about 2 or 3 minutes, or until the peanuts begin to turn into mush.

If you're using a blender you'll need to stop it once or twice to scrape down the sides and stir things up.

5

Stop the machine and add 1 tablespoon plus 1 teaspoon **oil.** Buzz the machine (press the button on and off) a few more times until the oil is mixed in.

6

Ask an adult to do this step.

Use as much as you want right away, then scrape the rest of the peanut butter into a jar or a container with a lid. Keep it in the refrigerator.

TIME TO EAT!

Apple-Yogurt Salad

You won't believe how good it tastes when you put a maple-yogurt sauce on apples. You also won't believe how easy this salad is to make. The main work is cutting the apples. Take your time doing that, and maybe invite a friend to do it with you. Then you can eat this yummy dish together for lunch or a snack.

INGREDIENTS:

- **2 cups plain yogurt**
- **$1/4$ cup real maple syrup**
- **1 lemon, cut in half**
- **5 medium-sized apples (your favorite kind)**

EXTRAS (YOU CHOOSE):

- **2 stalks celery, minced (cut in tiny pieces)**
- **$1/2$ cup raisins**
- **$1/2$ cup dried cranberries**
- **$1/2$ cup chopped, toasted walnuts**

YIELD: This recipe makes 4 or 5 servings.

TIME: It takes about 30 minutes to make, start to finish.

YOU WILL ALSO NEED:

- 2-cup liquid measure
- Medium-sized bowl
- Citrus juicer
- Large bowl
- Cutting board
- Small sharp knife for cutting apples (and celery, if using)
- Spoon for mixing
- Small bowls for the "extras"
- Bowls and spoons or forks for serving

ASK AN ADULT FOR HELP WITH:

- *Toasting walnuts ahead of time*
- *Cutting out the apple cores*

1

Measure 2 cups **yogurt.** Put it in a medium-sized bowl.

2

Measure 1/4 cup **maple syrup.** Add this to the yogurt and stir until the syrup is all mixed in.

3

Squeeze a **lemon** and pour the juice into a large bowl.

4

Cut the **apples** into quarters.

Ask an adult to cut out the seed area (core) of each quarter.

Then cut the apples into little chunks (the size of dice). Add them to the lemon juice, and stir to get the apples all wet.

The lemon juice keeps them from turning brown.

5

Pour the **yogurt mixture** into the apples and mix gently.

6

Put the **celery, raisins, dried cranberries,** and/or **walnuts** into small bowls and put them on the table.

These will be the toppings.

7

Serve the apple-yogurt salad in bowls.

Pass the toppings so each person can make his or hers special.

TIME TO EAT!

TOSSED GREEN SALAD

WITH TWO DRESSINGS

Some afternoon when you would like something interesting to do, why not turn your family kitchen into a salad laboratory? Ask a parent to take you to the farmers' market (if there's one in your community), or just ask to go to the grocery store and pick out an assortment of vegetables, "extras," and salad dressing ingredients. Then go home and get busy.

First, choose a dressing: Ranch Dressing or Apple Juice Vinaigrette. Make the dressing and then decide which vegetables you'd like to put into the salad (in addition to the salad greens), and wash and cut or grate them. Use any amount you like. Next, check out the list of extras, and get these ready as well. (Don't forget to look in the refrigerator for things like leftover cooked rice or couscous, potatoes, beans, or pasta, which are all very good in salads.) You can put everything in bowls and set up a salad bar for your family, or just toss the extras into the salad in one big bowl.

Next, you'll need to clean the salad greens. Make a "bath" of cold water in the sink or a big bowl, add the lettuce and spinach leaves, and swish them around. Dry them in a salad spinner or shake them in a colander and pat them dry with paper towels. Break the leaves into bite-sized pieces and put them in a large bowl. Drizzle the salad with dressing and toss with salad servers until all of the greens are coated. Be sure to pass around some extra dressing in a bowl in case people want more.

INGREDIENTS FOR THE SALAD (YOU CHOOSE):

- Lettuce, cleaned and dried (several kinds mixed together or just one kind)

- Spinach, stemmed, cleaned, and dried

- Carrots, peeled and grated or sliced

- Cucumbers, peeled and sliced

- Green, yellow, or red bell peppers, cored, seeded, and cut in strips

- Scallions, minced (trim the "hairy" tip, and cut white and lower half of green part in tiny pieces)

- Red cabbage, grated

- Alfalfa sprouts

- Cherry tomatoes, whole or halved

- About 2 tablespoons of dressing for each serving

EXTRAS (YOU CAN HAVE FUN WITH THESE!):

- Chopped olives

- Grated cheese (any kind)

- Strips of savory baked tofu (available in natural foods stores)

- Crispy croutons (page 36)

- Crunchy Chinese noodles (available in grocery stores)

- Toasted sunflower seeds or cashews

- Cooked pasta

- Leftover cooked grains (especially couscous)

- Chunks of cooked potatoes or beets

- Chickpeas or beans (Rinse and drain them in a strainer over the sink if they're canned.)

Sprouts

YOU WILL ALSO NEED:

- Small, sharp knife and cutting board for various things

- Possibly a vegetable peeler

- Possibly a grater

- Small bowls for extras, if making a salad bar

- Sink or big bowl for washing greens

- Salad spinner or colander

- Paper towels

- Salad bowl and servers

- Measuring spoons for dressing

- Plates and forks

Should you ask an adult for help making the salad or the dressings?

That's up to you, but make sure there is an adult in the house who knows you are doing this and can help you set up. (And, of course, if there is any task you feel uncomfortable doing, ask for help.)

RANCH DRESSING

INGREDIENTS:

- **2 tablespoons mayonnaise**
- **6 tablespoons buttermilk**
- **1 teaspoon cider vinegar**
- **$^1/_8$ teaspoon salt**
- **$^1/_2$ teaspoon onion powder**
- **$^1/_4$ teaspoon garlic powder**

YIELD: This recipe makes $^1/_2$ cup. (That's enough for 3 or 4 servings of salad or for 2 or 3 people to dip vegetables for a snack.)

TIME: It takes only 5 minutes to make, start to finish.

YOU WILL ALSO NEED:

- Measuring spoons
- Medium-small bowl
- Spoon or small whisk

NOTE: Ranch Dressing keeps for a week in the refrigerator if stored in a tightly covered container.

"My mom's getting mighty tired of making salad dressing every night. Now I can make this for her and give her a rest."
—Laura

1

Put in a medium-small bowl:
  2 tablespoons **mayonnaise**
  6 tablespoons **buttermilk**
  1 teaspoon **cider vinegar**
  $^1/_8$ teaspoon **salt**
  $^1/_2$ teaspoon **onion powder**
  $^1/_4$ teaspoon **garlic powder**

2

Mix well with a spoon or a small whisk.

3

Put the dressing on the salad, or put the bowl on the table and use it to dip all kinds of raw or lightly steamed vegetables.

TIME TO EAT!

APPLE JUICE VINAIGRETTE

INGREDIENTS:

- 4 tablespoons olive oil
- 2 tablespoons cider vinegar
- $^1/_2$ cup apple juice
- $^1/_4$ teaspoon salt
- $^1/_2$ teaspoon minced garlic
  (cut in tiny pieces)

YIELD: This recipe makes about $^3/_4$ cup.
(That's enough for 4 to 6 servings of salad.)

TIME: It takes about 10 minutes to make,
start to finish.

YOU WILL ALSO NEED:

- Measuring spoons
- Cutting board and a small, sharp knife
  for the garlic
- Small jar with a lid that fits tightly

NOTE: Apple Juice Vinaigrette keeps for
months in a tightly-covered jar in the
refrigerator.

1

Put into a jar:
  4 tablespoons **olive oil**
  2 tablespoons **cider vinegar**
  $^1/_2$ cup **apple juice**
  $^1/_4$ teaspoon **salt**
  $^1/_2$ teaspoon **garlic**

2

Put the top on tightly!

Shake!

3

Shake it again before you put it on
the salad.

TIME TO EAT!

EASY PASTA SALAD

Pasta salad is simply pasta and vegetables mixed with a delicious dressing. In this case, the dressing is your own Apple Juice Vinaigrette (page 59).

INGREDIENTS:

- 2 cups cooked pasta (tubes, macaroni, small shells, or twists)
- Half a red bell pepper, minced (cut in tiny pieces)
- 1 scallion, minced (cut in tiny pieces)
- 2 tablespoons chopped black olives
- 6 tablespoons Apple Juice Vinaigrette (page 59)
- Salt and pepper in shakers

YIELD: This recipe makes 2 to 3 servings.

TIME: It takes 20 minutes (including pasta cooking time), start to finish.

YOU WILL ALSO NEED:

- Medium-sized bowl
- Cutting board and small, sharp knife
- Measuring spoons
- Wooden spoon
- Plates and forks

NOTE TO THE ADULT:

Cook 1 cup (1/4 pound) pasta in boiling, salted water until tender. Drain it in a colander, rinse under cold running water, and drain again. Transfer to the medium-sized bowl.

1

You have the **cooked pasta** already in the bowl.

Add the **bell pepper, scallion,** and **olives.** Mix them in with the pasta, gently with a wooden spoon.

2

Shake the jar of **Apple Juice Vinaigrette.** Open it and measure out 6 tablespoons, one at a time, pouring each into the pasta.

Stir again with a wooden spoon.

3

Add a few shakes of **salt** and **pepper,** stir again, and serve warm or cool.

TIME TO EAT!

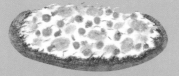

CHAPTER 3

MAIN AND SIDE DISHES: HELPING WITH DINNER FOR REAL

NOT-FROM-A-BOX
Macaroni
and
Cheese

For all of you macaroni and cheese fans out there, here is the real thing! Instead of just sprinkling some bright orange powder from a package into hot macaroni and mixing it in, here you make a genuine cheese sauce from scratch, just like a real chef. Then you mix it with cooked macaroni (which an adult should cook and drain for you ahead of time), sprinkle extra cheese on top, and bake it in the oven until it is bubbly. You will love this!

Don't be afraid of the dry mustard in the recipe. Even if you don't like the kind of mustard that some people like to put on sandwiches and hot dogs, you'll find that this mustard is not too spicy. It just gives the cheese an extra flavor boost, and the whole thing will taste really good because of it. (A couple of the kids said, "Eeuuu—mustard!" when we tested the recipe, but they loved the result.)

The cheese sauce in this recipe can also be made on its own, without the pasta. Make it for dinner some night to put on whatever vegetables your parents are cooking. It's especially good on asparagus, broccoli, cauliflower, and potatoes.

NOTE: Give yourself extra time during the set-up to grate the cheddar cheese. If you want, you can ask an adult to help you grate it in the food processor, but doing it by hand is really fun, and you will feel very accomplished. Watch your knuckles!

INGREDIENTS:

- 1/2 pound (2 cups) uncooked macaroni or baby pasta shells (4 cups cooked pasta)
- 2 tablespoons butter plus extra butter for the pan
- 2 cups milk
- 2 tablespoons unbleached white flour
- 2 teaspoons dry mustard
- 1 packed cup grated sharp cheddar cheese
- 1/3 cup grated parmesan cheese
- Extra cheddar for the top and for sprinkling onto each serving

YIELD: This recipe makes 5 or 6 servings.

TIME: It takes about 40 minutes to make and another 20 minutes to bake. That's about 1 hour, start to finish.

YOU WILL ALSO NEED:

- Handheld grater or food processor fitted with the grating attachment for grating the cheese ahead of time
- Large pot and a colander for cooking and draining the pasta
- Gratin pan or baking dish (2-quart size)
- Paper towel or waxed paper for buttering the pan
- 2-cup liquid measure
- Medium-sized pot or a bowl for heating the milk
- Dinner knife for cutting the butter
- Medium-sized saucepan
- Measuring cups and spoons
- Whisk
- Long-handled wooden spoon
- Rubber spatula
- Timer with a bell
- Plates and forks

ASK AN ADULT FOR HELP WITH:

- *Grating the cheese in a food processor, if using*
- *Cooking and draining the macaroni or shells*
- *Turning on the oven*
- *Helping to decide when the milk is hot enough*
- *Helping pour the hot cheese sauce into the pasta*
- *Putting the baking dish into the oven and taking it out*

NOTE TO THE ADULT:

To cook the macaroni, add 2 cups (1/2 pound) uncooked macaroni or small shells to a pot of boiling water. Stir, and boil for 5 to 8 minutes or until tender. Drain in a colander.

1

Ask an adult to cook 2 cups macaroni or tiny shells, and then to drain it and set it aside.

2

Also ask an adult to turn on the oven to 350°F.

Rub a little soft **butter** onto the insides of the baking pan, using a paper towel or waxed paper.

3

Measure 2 cups **milk**.

4

Heat the milk in a bowl in a microwave on **high** for 1 1/2 minutes. (You can also heat it in a pot over **low** heat on the stove. It should be very warm, but not boiling.)

Ask an adult to help decide when it's ready.

Put the warm milk aside for now.

5

Use a dinner knife to cut 2 tablespoons butter. Each line on the butter wrapper means 1 tablespoon.

6

Put the butter in a medium-sized saucepan and put the pot on the stove. Turn on the heat to **low**.

7

While the butter is melting, measure 2 tablespoons **flour** and 2 teaspoons **dry mustard** into a small bowl.

8

Sprinkle the flour and mustard into the **melted butter.**

Whisk until there are no more lumps.

9

Whisk and cook the **butter-flour-mustard mixture** for 30 seconds.

10

A two-person job:

- One person slowly pours the warm milk into the butter-flour-mustard a little at a time.

- The other person whisks the mixture as the milk is drizzled in.

11

Turn up the heat to **medium-low.** Cook the sauce for 3 minutes, whisking often. It will get thicker.

12

Sprinkle in 1 cup **cheddar** and 1/3 cup **parmesan.**

Cook the sauce for 1 more minute, stirring with a long-handled wooden spoon. The cheese will melt.

13

Put the cooked **macaroni** or **shells** into a big bowl. Carefully pour the hot cheese sauce into the pasta. **You might need adult help.**

Stir slowly from the bottom of the bowl with the long-handled spoon until the sauce is all mixed in.

14

Another two-person job:

- One person holds the big bowl, tilting it toward the buttered baking dish.

- Using the spatula, the other person scrapes all the stuff into the baking dish and spreads it in place.

15

Sprinkle a little extra cheese on top.

Ask an adult to put the pan in the oven.

Set the timer for 20 minutes.

Ask an adult to take the pan out.

TIME TO EAT!

A big pan of steaming hot lasagna comes out of the oven and all of a sudden your house smells like a great Italian restaurant. The most amazing part of this whole situation is that you are the one who made it!

In many lasagna recipes, the noodles are cooked ahead of time, and they are soft and slippery. This recipe is different. You get to use uncooked noodles, which are stiff and easy to handle. They will soften completely in the oven because the moisture from the tomato sauce and the ricotta cheese will heat up and cook them.

This lasagna has a built-in pesto flavor, because you put a lot of fresh basil and garlic into the ricotta mixture. This is a very neat trick.

For the tomato sauce, use your favorite brand. You'll need a 26-ounce jar, which is a little more than 3 cups of sauce. And, because people often like extra sauce in (or on) their lasagna, think about having a second jar on hand so you can put a little extra on the final layer (Step 14), or just heat some up and serve extra at the table. While the lasagna is baking, you can make some Garlic Bread (page 160) or a Tossed Green Salad (page 56) to serve with it.

This makes a large batch, so it's great for a party or a family gathering. If you make it for a smaller group and you have some left over, tell your parents they can freeze it and defrost and reheat it another time.

NOTE: Mozzarella cheese is easier to grate when it's cold or if it is the harder (rather than the softer) kind. You can grate it by hand, or ask an adult to help you use the food processor with the grating attachment.

"It gets very bubbly so you know it's done." —Arie

INGREDIENTS:

- 2 pounds ricotta cheese (4 cups)
- 20 fresh basil leaves
- 1 tablespoon minced (cut in tiny pieces) or crushed garlic
- 1 cup grated parmesan cheese
- A 26-ounce jar of tomato sauce (a generous 3 cups)
- 12 lasagna noodles (about 3/4 pound)
- 1 pound mozzarella cheese, grated (4 packed cups)

YIELD: This recipe makes about 16 servings.

TIME: It takes about 45 minutes to make, and almost an hour to bake. Then it needs to cool for 15 minutes. Figure on about 2 hours, start to finish.

YOU WILL ALSO NEED:

- Small, sharp knife (or a garlic press) and a cutting board for mincing (or crushing) the garlic ahead of time
- Handheld grater or food processor fitted with the grating attachment for grating the mozzarella ahead of time
- Large bowl
- Scissors
- Measuring cups and spoons
- Long-handled spoon or fork
- 1-cup liquid measure
- 9 by 13-inch baking pan
- Soup spoon
- Aluminum foil
- Timer with a bell
- Knife and spatula for serving
- Plates and forks

ASK AN ADULT FOR HELP WITH:

- *Setting up the food processor (if using) and taking the grated cheese out of it*
- *Turning on the oven*
- *Covering the pan tightly with foil*
- *Putting the pan into the oven and taking it out*
- *Lifting the foil during the baking and sprinkling on the extra parmesan*

1

Ask an adult to turn on the oven to 375°F.

2

Put the **ricotta cheese** into a large bowl.

3

Make a little pile of 20 **basil leaves.** Hold them tightly together and snip them into the bowl with scissors. Snip them really small.

4

Add 1 tablespoon **garlic** and 1/2 cup of the **parmesan.**

You will use the rest of the parmesan for the top.

5

Mix well with a long-handled spoon or a big fork. You have just made the **ricotta mixture.** Set this aside for now.

6

Measure 1 cup **tomato sauce.** Pour it into the baking pan and spread it a little with the back of a spoon.

7

Put a layer of **noodles** on the sauce. They should touch edges, but should not overlap too much.

8

Use a soup spoon to put blobs of the ricotta mixture onto the noodles. The blobs do not need to connect or touch.

Use about half the ricotta mixture.

9 Measure another cup of sauce. Pour it over the blobs of cheese and the noodles and spread it a little.

10 Sprinkle on about half of the **mozzarella.**

11 Put another layer of noodles right on top of the cheese.

12 Put the rest of the ricotta mixture on top of the noodles, in blobs, like before.

13 Sprinkle the rest of the mozzarella over everything.

14 Pour on the rest of the sauce and spread it a little.

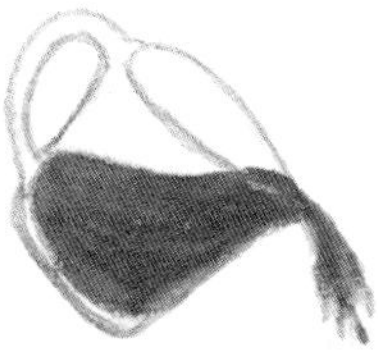

15 Cover the pan tightly with a big piece of foil. **Ask an adult to help with the foil, and with putting the pan in the oven.**

Set the timer for 40 minutes.

16 Ask an adult to do all of this:

After 40 minutes, take the pan from the oven, remove the foil, and sprinkle the top with $1/2$ cup parmesan. Bake, uncovered, for 15 minutes longer, and then take it out of the oven.

17 Let it cool for 15 minutes before serving.

TIME TO EAT!

vegetarian FRIED RICE

Fried rice is basically stir-fried vegetables with cooked rice added. Then it's all fried up together until it looks like the rice is sprinkled through and through with colorful little tidbits. Often, fried rice also contains pieces of cooked meat and scrambled egg. This special vegetarian version has tofu instead of the meat, but you don't have to be a vegetarian to like it!

Chopping vegetables can be fun, especially with the help of a sibling or a friend. You will need to chop carrots, broccoli, zucchini, garlic, and scallions ahead of time. You will also cut tofu into tiny pieces and slice water chestnuts, if the ones you're using are not pre-sliced in the can. Your parents can help make the vegetable preparation easier by cutting the carrots, broccoli, and zucchini into strips first. Once that is done, you can chop up the vegetables. But always take your time and go slowly when you're using a knife, and keep your eyes on your hands the whole time.

INGREDIENTS:

- 2 eggs
- 1 tablespoon plus 1 teaspoon canola or peanut oil
- 2 cups sliced carrots
- 2 cups chopped broccoli
- Salt in a shaker
- 1/2 pound firm tofu, cut into small cubes, like dice
- 1 small zucchini, cut into small cubes, like dice
- 1 1/2 teaspoons minced (cut in tiny pieces) or crushed garlic
- 1 cup peas
- 4 scallions, sliced (trim the "hairy" tip, and cut the white and lower half of the green part in very thin slices)
- 1 (8-ounce) can water chestnuts, drained and sliced
- 4 cups cooked rice (white or brown)
- A few drops of soy sauce (as much as tastes good to you)
- A few drops of sesame oil (as much as tastes good to you)

YIELD: This recipe makes 5 or 6 servings.

TIME: It takes about 30 minutes to set up and about 15 minutes to cook. That's 45 minutes, start to finish.

YOU WILL ALSO NEED:

- Sharp knife (and maybe a garlic press) and a cutting board for preparing the vegetables ahead of time
- Small bowl and fork for the eggs
- Frying pan
- Measuring cups and spoons
- Spatula
- Plate
- Paper towels
- Long-handled wooden spoon
- Dinner knife
- Plates and forks

ASK AN ADULT FOR HELP WITH:

- *Cooking the rice*
- *Taking the frying pan off the stove after you cook the eggs and wiping the pan clean*
- *Stir-frying*

NOTE TO THE ADULT:

This recipe calls for 4 cups of cooked rice. Put 1¹/₂ cups white or brown rice and 2¹/₂ cups water in a saucepan. Bring to a boil, then cover and lower the heat to the slowest possible simmer. White rice will be ready in 20 minutes; brown rice takes 40 to 45 minutes and might need a few tablespoons of additional water. Fluff the rice with a fork when it is done to let steam escape and to make it fluffy.

"People could not like plain tofu and still like this a LOT!" —Eve

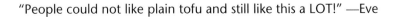

1

Break 2 **eggs** into a small bowl. Beat them with a fork until they are completely yellow and smooth.

2

Put a frying pan on the stove. Add 1 teaspoon **oil,** and then turn on the heat to **medium.** Wait for 30 seconds.

3

Add the beaten eggs and use a spatula to slowly push them around in the pan until there are no more wet areas.

Use the spatula to lift the eggs out of the pan and put them on a plate.

4

Ask an adult to take the pan off the heat and wipe it clean with a paper towel.

Put the clean pan back on the stove and add 1 tablespoon oil.

5

Turn on the heat to **medium-high** and wait for 30 seconds. Add the **carrots,** the **broccoli,** and a few shakes of **salt.**

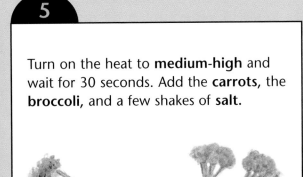

6

With the wooden spoon, stir and cook over **medium-high** heat for 3 minutes.

Ask an adult to help if the air above the pan feels too hot.

7

Add the **tofu, zucchini,** and **garlic.** Cook and stir for 2 more minutes.

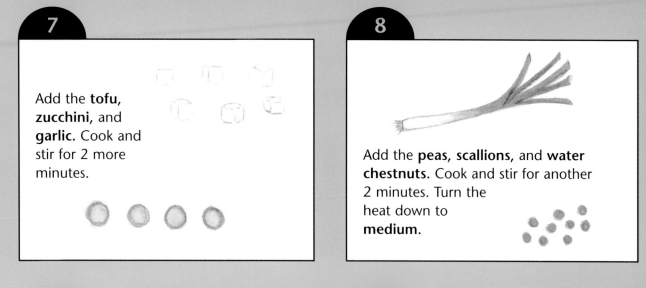

8

Add the **peas, scallions,** and **water chestnuts.** Cook and stir for another 2 minutes. Turn the heat down to **medium.**

9

A two-person job:

- One person holds the container of cooked **rice.**
- The other person slowly scrapes it into the pan of vegetables and tofu.

10

Carefully stir the rice into the vegetables. It helps if you gently scoop up the vegetables from the bottom and turn them on top of the rice about 10 or 12 times. **You might want to ask an adult for help.**

11

Remember the cooked eggs from earlier? Use a dinner knife to cut them into small pieces right on the plate, and then scrape them into the rice. Gently stir them in.

12

Scoop the fried rice onto serving plates. Pass around a bottle of **soy sauce** and one of **sesame oil,** too. Let everyone shake a few drops of these onto his or her own portion.

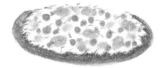

TIME TO EAT!

You tear up a bunch of corn tortillas and put them in a baking pan with cheese. Then you mix up some buttermilk and eggs, pour it over the top, and bake the whole thing in the oven. When it comes out, you have this great-tasting main dish for lunch or dinner. It's that easy! (In Mexico they have a dish similar to this, called "chilaquiles." It was invented to use up leftover tortillas.)

The biggest job here is grating a lot of cheese beforehand, but that can be fun if you have a friend keeping you company, or if an adult helps you do it in the food processor with the grating attachment.

Torn Tortilla Casserole goes very well with salsa and salad. If you have the time, you can put together some Real Salsa (page 154) or a Tossed Green Salad (page 56) while the casserole bakes.

INGREDIENTS:

- **Can of vegetable oil cooking spray or canola oil for the pan**
- **12 corn tortillas**
- **2 cups grated Monterey jack cheese (about 1/2 pound)**
- **4 eggs**
- **3/4 teaspoon salt**
- **2 cups buttermilk**
- **Paprika for the top**

TO PUT ON TOP OR ON THE SIDE WHEN YOU EAT IT (YOU CHOOSE):

- **Salsa (as much as you like)**
- **Sour cream (as much as you like)**

YIELD: This recipe makes 5 or 6 servings.

TIME: It takes about 20 minutes to make (depending on how long it takes you to grate the cheese) and 40 minutes to bake. That's about 1 hour, start to finish.

YOU WILL ALSO NEED:

- Handheld grater or food processor fitted with the grating attachment for grating the cheese ahead of time

- Brush for painting the pan with oil, if using

- 9 by 13-inch baking pan

- Large mixing bowl

- Measuring spoons

- 2-cup liquid measure

- Whisk

- Rubber spatula

- Timer with a bell

- Knife and spatula for serving

- Plates and forks

ASK AN ADULT FOR HELP WITH:

- *Setting up the food processor (if using) and taking the grated cheese out of it*

- *Turning on the oven*

- *Putting the pan into the oven and taking it out*

1

Ask an adult to turn on the oven to 350°F.

Spray the pan with **oil spray,** or paint it with a little **oil.**

2

Tear **6 tortillas** into bite-sized pieces and put them here and there in the pan, spreading them out so they cover the bottom.

3

Sprinkle half of the **cheese** on top of the tortillas, covering all of the surfaces.

4

Tear 6 more tortillas and put them here and there on top of the cheese.

5

Sprinkle the rest of the cheese over the top.

6

Break 4 **eggs** into a large bowl.

7

Measure 3/4 teaspoon **salt** and sprinkle it into the eggs.

8

Measure 2 cups **buttermilk** and pour it into the eggs.

9

Beat the mixture with a whisk until it is all one color and you don't see any more yolks.

10

A two-person job:

- One person holds the bowl, tilting it toward the pan, and slowly pours in the wet mixture.

- The other person scrapes the wet mixture in and spreads it in place with a rubber spatula.

11

Sprinkle the top with a little **paprika** to give it a nice color.

PAPRIKA↓

12

Ask an adult to put it in the oven.

Set the timer for 40 minutes.

13

Ask an adult to take the casserole out.

Cut it into squares and serve hot, with **salsa** and **sour cream**.

TIME TO EAT!

Tell your parents not to throw away the leftover spaghetti the next time they serve it for dinner. In fact, ask them to make about half a pound extra so you can have leftovers on purpose. Why? Because it's time for Spaghetti Pie!

This recipe is like making a pie and pizza and spaghetti all at the same time. You mix the leftover spaghetti with sauce and cheese, add a few extra ingredients if you choose, and bake it in a pie pan until it's crispy on top. Then you cut it into wedge-shaped pieces that you can eat with your hands. It's hard to make a mistake with this recipe, so just relax and have a good time.

Here's what some of the kids who tested this recipe had to say about it:

"This spaghetti is kind of not normal."
—Irene

"Silly me! I thought it was going to be dessert!" —Eve

"You have to eat it over a plate, because pieces might fall off." —Liat

INGREDIENTS:

- 1 tablespoon olive oil
- 4 cups cooked spaghetti ($^1/_2$ pound uncooked)
- 1$^1/_2$ cups tomato sauce (half a 26-ounce jar)
- $^1/_2$ cup grated parmesan cheese
- 10 fresh basil leaves
- $^1/_2$ cup grated mozzarella or Monterey jack cheese

EXTRAS (YOU CHOOSE):

- A handful of sliced black olives
- 10 mushrooms, cleaned and sliced
- $^1/_2$ cup bell pepper slices

YIELD: This recipe makes about 4 servings.

TIME: It takes about 15 minutes to prepare and another 30 minutes to bake. That's a total of 45 minutes, start to finish.

YOU WILL ALSO NEED:

- Handheld grater or food processor fitted with the grating attachment for grating the cheese ahead of time
- Small, sharp knife and a cutting board for preparing the extras, if you choose them, ahead of time
- Measuring cups and spoons
- Deep 10-inch pie pan
- Brush for painting oil in the pan
- Large bowl
- Scissors
- 2-cup liquid measure
- Long-handled spoon or fork
- Rubber spatula
- Timer with a bell
- Knife and spatula for serving
- Plates and forks

ASK AN ADULT FOR HELP WITH:

- *Cooking and draining the spaghetti ahead of time*
- *Turning on the oven*
- *Setting up the food processor and taking the cheese out of it*
- *Putting the pan into the oven and taking it out*
- *Cutting the pie into wedges*

NOTE TO THE ADULT:

To cook the spaghetti, add $1/2$ pound spaghetti to a pot of boiling water. Stir, and boil for 5 to 8 minutes or until tender. Drain in a colander.

1

Ask an adult to turn on the oven to 350°F.

2

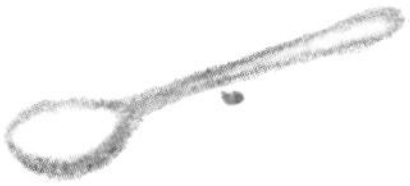

Measure 1 tablespoon **olive oil** and pour it into a pie pan. Brush it around.

3

Measure 4 cups **cooked spaghetti** and put it in a large bowl.

4

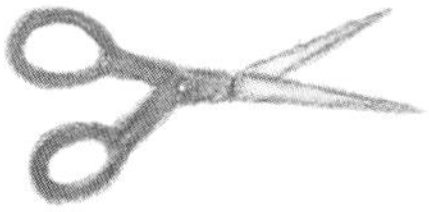

Use a scissors to snip the spaghetti in the bowl into smaller pieces.

5

Measure 1^1/$_2$ cups **tomato sauce** and pour it into the spaghetti.

6

Measure ^{1}/$_2$ cup **parmesan** and sprinkle it in.

7

Make a little pile of 10 **basil leaves.** Hold the leaves tightly together over the bowl and snip them into tiny pieces with scissors. Let the pieces fall right into the bowl.

If you'd like, you can also add:

the **olives**

the **mushrooms**

1/2 cup **bell pepper** slices

Stir everything together with a long-handled spoon or fork.

Stir it slowly, so it won't splash.

A two-person job:

- One person holds the bowl, tilting it toward the pie pan.
- The other person scrapes the spaghetti mixture into the pie pan with a rubber spatula and pats it into place.

Sprinkle the top with 1/2 cup **mozzarella** or **jack cheese.**

Ask an adult to put it in the oven.

Set the timer for 30 minutes.

Ask an adult to take it out of the oven and cut it into wedges.

Blow on it before taking a bite!

TIME TO EAT!

LITTLE PIZZAS WITH HOMEMADE CRUST

Goodbye soggy, doughy, pizza-shaped objects. Hello crispy, homemade crusts, and the best (and the most real) pizza you've ever had! You will want to make this again and again, and your family will want you to, also.

NOTES: Mozzarella cheese is easier to grate when it's cold, or if it is the harder, rather than the softer, kind. You can grate it by hand, or ask an adult to help you use the food processor fitted with the grating attachment.

This pizza dough has yeast in it. Yeast is a powdery ingredient that "wakes up" when it is dissolved in water. Once it is added to dough, it makes the dough puff up and grow to nearly twice its size! The yeast only works when the water it is dissolved in isn't too hot. Check to be sure the water is the same temperature as you. (Do a little test by sticking a clean pinky into the water. It should feel neither hot nor cold but just slightly warm.)

INGREDIENTS:

- 1 cup lukewarm water
- 1 teaspoon active dry yeast
- 2 tablespoons olive oil
- 2½ cups bread flour, plus extra for handling the dough
- 1 teaspoon salt
- Cornmeal for the baking tray

TOPPINGS (YOU CHOOSE):

- About 1 cup tomato sauce (maybe more)
- About ½ cup pesto (store-bought or homemade)
- ¾ cup sliced black olives
- 12 mushrooms, thinly sliced
- 1 green bell pepper, thinly sliced
- About 1½ cups grated mozzarella cheese

YIELD: This recipe makes six 6-inch pizzas.

TIME: It takes about 10 minutes to make the dough, 1 hour to rest the dough, 15 minutes to shape the pizzas, and 15 to 20 minutes to bake them. Whew! That's just about 2 hours, start to finish.

YOU WILL ALSO NEED:

- 1-cup liquid measure
- Measuring cups and spoons
- Spoon for stirring
- Medium-sized bowl
- Food processor fitted with the steel blade
- Table with board or countertop ("work area")
- Clean kitchen towel
- Timer with a bell
- Small, sharp knife and a cutting board for preparing vegetable toppings
- Handheld grater or food processor fitted with the grating attachment for grating the cheese
- Large baking tray
- Scissors or pastry cutter for the dough
- Rolling pin (optional)
- Soup spoons for spreading sauces
- Pizza cutter or knife
- Plates and napkins

ASK AN ADULT FOR HELP WITH:

- *Setting up the food processor and taking the dough out of it*
- *Cutting the dough*
- *Turning on the oven*
- *Putting the tray into the oven and then taking it out and standing by while you put on the toppings*
- *Putting the tray back into the oven and taking it out at the end*
- *Taking the pizzas off the tray, and cutting them*

NOTES TO THE ADULT:

ABOUT STORING AND FREEZING THE DOUGH:
Pizza dough freezes beautifully for up to 3 months if stored in a sealed plastic bag. Defrost the frozen dough for at least 4 hours in the refrigerator or 2 hours at room temperature before using.

IF YOU DON'T HAVE A FOOD PROCESSOR:
Ideally, the kids should make the dough themselves (with some adult help), using a food processor. If you don't have one, here is a method for making the dough by hand. Hand-mixing bread dough is difficult for a child, so you will have to do most of it. But children can still do the measuring and kneading. The amounts are the same as listed.

Put the lukewarm water into a medium-large mixing bowl. Sprinkle in the yeast, stir, and let it stand for 5 minutes. Stir in 1 tablespoon of the olive oil. Add 1 cup of the flour and the salt, and beat with a whisk. Gradually add the remaining flour, mixing first with a wooden spoon and then with floured hands, until the dough comes together. (It will be soft.) Add just enough flour to keep it from being very sticky. Turn out the dough onto a floured work area and knead for about 5 minutes. Clean out the bowl and add the other tablespoon olive oil to the clean bowl.

Proceed with Step 8 of the recipe (page 85).

1

PART 1: MAKING THE DOUGH

Measure 1 cup **lukewarm water.**

"Lukewarm" means that when you dip your clean pinky into the water it should feel no warmer or cooler than your pinky. Let it cool down for a few minutes if it's too warm.

2

Measure 1 teaspoon **yeast** and sprinkle it into the water in the measuring cup. Stir to mix it up.

Measure 1 tablespoon **olive oil** and pour this into the **water-yeast mixture.**

3

Measure another tablespoon olive oil and put it in a medium-sized bowl.

Put the bowl aside.

4

Measure 2^1/$_2$ cups **flour** and 1 teaspoon **salt.** Carefully pour these into the container of the food processor.

5

Turn on the food processor. As it runs, pour all of the water-yeast mixture in through the feed tube.

6

Keep the food processor running. In just a few seconds the water will have turned the flour into dough.

7

Leave the dough in the food processor for a minute while you sprinkle some flour onto the work area. Also, rub some flour into the palms of your clean hands.

8

Ask an adult to take the dough out of the food processor and put it on the work area where you sprinkled the flour.

The dough will be a little sticky. Push it together into a smooth ball, rubbing more flour into your hands if you need to. Push the dough around and into itself for about 2 or 3 minutes.

9

Put the ball of dough into the bowl with the olive oil in it. Swish the dough around, then turn it upside-down and put it back in the bowl.

9½

Cover the bowl with a clean kitchen towel and let the dough rest for about 1 hour. (You could set the timer.)
It will puff up a lot during this time. You can prepare the toppings while you wait.

10

When the dough has finished resting, ask an adult to turn on the oven to 450°F.

Sprinkle a large baking tray with a handful or two of **cornmeal** (enough to lightly cover the surface).

11

Lift the dough out of the bowl and put it on the work area. Cut it into 6 similar pieces with scissors or a pastry cutter.

You might need an adult to help.

12

Use your hands to slowly stretch each piece into a 6-inch circle or oval.

It's okay if the dough tears a little or if it ends up a slightly odd shape. (You can also just make balls and roll them into 6-inch circles with a rolling pin.)

NOT TIME TO EAT YET! TURN THE PAGE...

13

Carefully put the circles on the tray on top of the cornmeal.

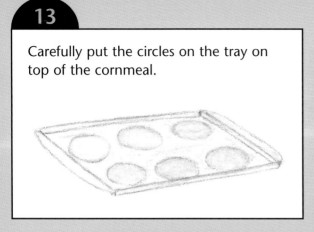

14

PART 2: BAKING THE PIZZAS

Ask an adult to put the tray in the oven.

Set the timer for 8 minutes.

15

While the dough is baking, take out your toppings and have them ready.

Ask an adult to take the tray out of the oven and to stand by.

16

Use a soup spoon to spread some sauce onto each pizza. A good amount for either:

> 2 to 3 tablespoons
> **tomato sauce**

> or

> 1 to 2 tablespoons
> **pesto**

17

After spreading the sauce or pesto, you might like to put on some sliced **olives**, **peppers,** or **mushrooms**. Sprinkle with a handful or two of **cheese**. Careful! The tray is hot!

18

Ask an adult to put the tray back in the oven for 5 to 8 more minutes, and then to take it out. An adult should also take the pizzas off the tray, put them on plates or a board, and cut them.

Wait a few minutes for the cheese to cool off.

TIME TO EAT!

Tortillas BY HAND

(Plain or filled)

A flour tortilla is made with only three ingredients: flour, salt, and water, mixed together until they form a dough. Shape the dough into little balls with your hands, then roll each ball into a thin, floppy circle with a rolling pin. The tortillas are cooked, one at a time, in a frying pan on the stove. You can eat them plain, or fill them with refried beans and/or some cheese and/or a little salsa. Try the Real Salsa on page 154, or just use a good store-bought kind.

INGREDIENTS:

- 1 cup unbleached white flour, plus extra for rolling the dough
- 1/4 teaspoon salt
- 1/2 cup water

EXTRAS FOR THE FILLING (YOU CHOOSE):

- A spoonful or two of refried beans for each serving
- A handful or two of grated Monterey jack or cheddar cheese for each serving
- Salsa (as much as you like)

YIELD: This recipe makes 4 tortillas.

TIME: It takes 10 to 15 minutes to make the dough, about 5 minutes to roll out each tortilla, and about 10 to 15 minutes more for each tortilla to cook. That's 40 to 50 minutes, start to finish.

YOU WILL ALSO NEED:

- Measuring cups and spoons
- Medium-large mixing bowl
- Fork or spoon for mixing
- 1-cup liquid measure
- Table with board or countertop ("work area")
- Rolling pin
- 12-inch ruler for measuring tortilla
- Frying pan
- Spatula
- Spoon for adding fillings, if using
- Plates

ASK AN ADULT FOR HELP WITH:

- *Rolling out the dough*
- *Cooking the tortillas*

87

1

Measure 1 cup **flour** and put it in a medium-large bowl.

2

Measure ¼ teaspoon **salt**. Sprinkle it into the flour and stir a little. Make a dent in the center with a spoon.

3

Measure ½ cup **water** and pour it into the dent.

4

Mix with a fork or spoon for about 1 minute, then rub some flour into the palms of your clean hands and use your hands to push the dough together until it becomes a smooth ball.

5

Sprinkle a little flour onto the work area. Put the dough on the floured area and divide it into 4 equal parts. Roll each part into a smaller ball.

6

Rub a little flour onto the rolling pin. Roll each ball until it becomes a very thin, flat circle about 6 or 7 inches across. You can measure it.

Take your time! **You may want to ask an adult for help.** Add more flour if it feels sticky.

7

Put a frying pan on the stove and place a **tortilla** in the pan. Turn on the heat to **medium.**

8

Cook on one side for 3 or 4 minutes, until it has golden brown spots underneath. (Use a spatula to peek and **ask an adult to help.**)

9

When the tortilla is ready, flip it over, and cook it on the other side.

If you want to eat it plain, just wait until it has golden brown spots on the second side and it's done!

If you want to fill it, go to the next step.

10

To make filled tortillas you can add:

a spoonful or two of **beans,** spread into place

a handful or two of **cheese**

a little **salsa**

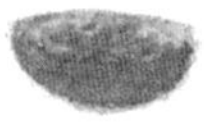

Put fillings on half of the circle.

11

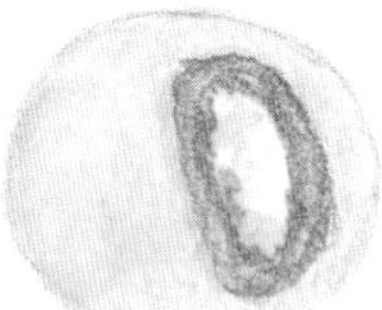

Use the spatula to fold over the plain half to cover the filling.

12

Cook the tortilla for a little longer, until the cheese melts. Use a spatula to lift it out of the pan and put it on a plate.

TIME TO EAT!

CARNIVAL BAKED POTATOES

WITH MILD RED PEPPER SAUCE

"Carnival Baked Potatoes is a lot like a salad bar, only hot." —Sam

"I love them with cheese and broccoli and that red pepper sauce. They're so, um, good." —Irene

"These potatoes make me really love being a recipe tester." —Zach

So what is a Carnival Baked Potato? It is a baked potato with a lot of different toppings set up in little bowls: broccoli, cheese, cottage cheese, sour cream, olives, and other goodies. An adult prepares the broccoli and bakes the potatoes, but *you* get to choose what to put on! The crowning touch is a delicious mild red pepper sauce that you can make yourself. The whole thing is very festive and colorful, like a carnival.

INGREDIENTS:

- 4 medium-sized russet potatoes, scrubbed
- 2 tablespoons butter to cook the broccoli (plus extra for serving with the potatoes)
- 2 cups chopped broccoli
- Salt and pepper in shakers
- 1 cup grated cheddar cheese
- 1 cup cottage cheese
- 1/2 cup sour cream
- 1/2 cup sliced black olives
- 1/4 cup minced (cut in tiny pieces) fresh chives or scallion tops (green part)
- Mild Red Pepper Sauce

YIELD: This recipe makes 4 generous servings.

TIME: It takes about 45 minutes to bake the potatoes. Everything else can be prepared during this time.

YOU WILL ALSO NEED:

- Small, sharp knife and a cutting board for preparing the vegetables
- Medium-sized pot with a lid
- 1-cup liquid measure
- Handheld grater or food processor fitted with the grating attachment for grating the cheese
- Measuring cups and spoons
- Small dishes for the various toppings
- Blender
- Medium-sized wire-mesh strainer, plus a bowl it fits over
- Soup spoon
- Forks, plates, and spoons

ASK AN ADULT FOR HELP WITH:

- *Preparing the broccoli*
- *Cutting the peppers*
- *Helping to decide when the peppers are ready*
- *Baking the potatoes, then taking them out of the oven and cutting them open*
- *Setting up the food processor (if using) and taking the grated cheese out of it*
- *Setting up the blender*

NOTES TO THE ADULT:

Your jobs are to bake the potatoes and cook the broccoli.

- To bake the potatoes: Preheat the oven to 400°F. Scrub 4 medium-sized russet potatoes, and pierce them a few times with a fork. Bake, unwrapped, directly on the oven rack, for about 45 to 50 minutes, or until tender.
- To prepare the broccoli: Melt 2 tablespoons butter in a medium-sized skillet. Add 2 cups broccoli, and salt lightly. Cover and cook until bright green and just tender, about 5 minutes.

MILD RED PEPPER SAUCE

It's the sign of a very good cook to know how to make a great-tasting sauce, and this one is definitely great-tasting. In fact, it's so good you might want to try it on other things, like grilled tofu, rice, or pasta.

INGREDIENTS:

- 2 medium-sized red bell peppers
- $1/2$ cup water
- $1/4$ teaspoon salt
- 1 small clove garlic, peeled

YIELD: This recipe makes a little less than 1 cup of sauce. (That is more than enough for 4 servings of Carnival Baked Potatoes.)

TIME: It takes about 10 minutes to make the sauce, start to finish.

1

Ask an adult to make the baked potatoes and to cook the broccoli.

While the potatoes are baking, you can make the Mild Red Pepper Sauce.

2

You might want adult help with this.

On a cutting board, cut 2 medium-sized **red bell peppers** in half the long way. Cut out the stem area and scrape out the white stuff and the seeds. Cut the peppers into 1-inch chunks.

3

Put the pepper chunks in a medium-sized pot.

Measure $1/2$ cup **water** and pour it in.

4

Cover the pot and put it on the stove. Turn on the heat to **medium-low** and cook for about 5 minutes, or until the peppers are soft.

Ask an adult to lift the lid and to help you decide if the peppers are ready.

5

Take the pot off the stove, and leave it uncovered for about 10 minutes.

The peppers need to cool down a little. During this time, get other things ready.

6

Put in separate, small dishes:

- 1 cup **cheddar cheese**
- 1 cup **cottage cheese**
- $1/2$ cup **sour cream**
- $1/2$ cup **black olives**
- 2 cups **broccoli** (that an adult has cooked for you)
- $1/4$ cup **chives** or **scallion greens**

7

Put all of the toppings on the table.

Also, put out **butter** and **salt** and **pepper** shakers.

8

Now, back to the sauce.

Put the cooled-down, cooked peppers into the blender with all of their liquid.

Add $1/4$ teaspoon salt and 1 small, peeled clove of **garlic**.

Blend until liquidy (about 40 seconds).

9

Put a medium-sized strainer over a bowl. Pour the blended peppers into the strainer and slowly stir it around with a soup spoon. Take your time.

Smooth sauce will drip into the bowl and the pepper skins will stay in the strainer. (You won't need them.)

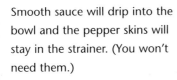

10

When all of the sauce has dripped into the bowl, put it on the table with the other toppings.

Don't forget the spoon for serving the sauce.

11

Now the table is set with all the yummy things you can choose to put on your potatoes.

When the potatoes are ready, ask an adult to bring them to the table, put them on serving plates, and cut them open.

12

Carefully mash the hot insides of the potatoes with a fork, and add some butter and cheddar, so they can melt. Then add other toppings any way you choose. Drizzle on some pepper sauce last. It will look beautiful!

TIME TO EAT!

Raw baby carrots make a wonderful snack, especially when you dip them in homemade Ranch Dressing (page 58). But sometimes it is nice to cook them in a little bit of flavored sauce. Then, instead of being just a snack, they can be a side dish for dinner.

As I'm sure you know, parents usually appreciate it when you help with dinner, especially when you have your own recipe and you really know what you're doing! This recipe is pretty much worry-free, because you use the carrots right out of the bag, with no cutting involved. And the coolest part of this recipe is that *you* are the boss of deciding when the carrots are done—*you* get to decide if they should be served crunchy or soft.

This recipe calls for vegetable broth. The flavor of the broth is important, so use a kind that tastes good to you. Ask your parents to buy several different kinds of vegetable broth for you to taste, so you can discover a brand you really like. I usually find my favorite brand of vegetable broth (called "Imagine") in the natural foods section of the grocery store. It's the kind that comes packed in a rectangular, one-quart "box" with a spout on top.

INGREDIENTS:
- **2 tablespoons butter**
- **¹/₂ teaspoon dried thyme**
- **1-pound bag baby carrots**
- **Salt in a shaker**
- **¹/₂ cup vegetable broth**

YIELD: This recipe makes 4 or 5 servings.

TIME: It takes about 15 minutes, start to finish.

YOU WILL ALSO NEED:
- Dinner knife for slicing butter
- Large frying pan with a lid
- Wooden spoon
- Measuring spoons
- 1-cup liquid measure
- Small spoon for tasting
- Plates and forks

ASK AN ADULT FOR HELP WITH:
- *Lifting the lid of the pan to see if the carrots are done (Hot steam will escape when the lid is lifted!)*

1

Use a dinner knife to cut 2 tablespoons **butter.** Each line on the butter wrapper means 1 tablespoon.

2

Put the butter in a large frying pan on the stove and turn on the heat to **medium-low.** Push the butter around with a wooden spoon until it is completely melted.

3

Measure ¹/₂ teaspoon **thyme** and sprinkle it in. Stir it around to flavor the butter.

4

Add the **carrots** and stir them around until they are completely coated with the flavored butter.

5

Sprinkle in about 3 shakes of **salt.**

Measure ¹/₂ cup **vegetable broth** and pour it in.

6

Cover the pan, and let the carrots cook for 5 to 10 minutes.

Ask an adult to lift the lid so you can taste a carrot and decide if it's ready.

Blow on it first!

7

Be sure to spoon some of the delicious sauce over each serving.

TIME TO EAT!

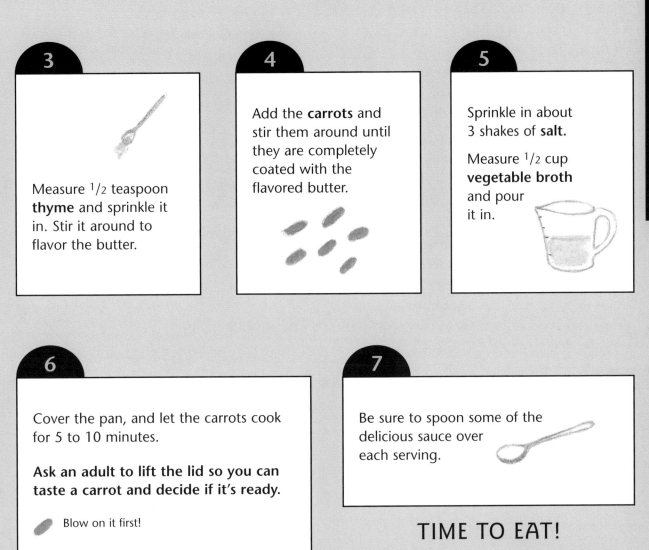

PEAS WITH BUTTER AND MINT

Cooked peas might seem ordinary at first glance. But look again! In this special recipe you cook them in melted butter with a little bit of a mint in it. There are two kinds of mint used here: dried mint, to flavor the butter, and fresh mint, to refresh and flavor your mouth. It's very unusual, and I think you will love it!

This recipe is easy because, of course, the peas don't need to be cut. (At least, I've never heard of cutting peas, unless you are a tiny elf.) If you are making this in the early summertime, when fresh sugar snap peas or snow peas are available, you can use them in this recipe instead of frozen regular peas. (Use 1 pound whole sugar snaps or snow peas. These are the kinds of peas where you can eat the whole pod, and it tastes very crunchy and sweet.)

NOTE: Another nice thing to do with fresh mint leaves: Put them in a glass of lemonade for a really refreshing drink.

INGREDIENTS:

- **1-pound package frozen peas**
- **1 to 2 tablespoons butter**
- **2 teaspoons dried mint**
- **Salt in a shaker**
- **10 fresh mint leaves**

YIELD: This recipe makes 4 servings.

TIME: It takes about 10 minutes to make, start to finish.

YOU WILL ALSO NEED:

- Large wire-mesh strainer with a bowl it fits over
- Dinner knife for slicing butter
- Large frying pan
- Wooden spoon
- Measuring spoons
- Scissors
- Plates and forks or spoons

Should you ask an adult for help?

That's up to you, but make sure there is an adult in the house who knows you are doing this, has read through the recipe with you ahead of time, and can help you set up. (And, of course, if there is any task you feel uncomfortable doing, ask for help.)

1

Put the **peas** in a large strainer. Hold them under a faucet and let warm tap water run over them for about 1 minute, until they are defrosted.

Put the strainer over a bowl so the water can drain off.

2

Use a dinner knife to cut 1 tablespoon **butter.** Each line on the butter wrapper means 1 tablespoon.

3

Put the butter in a large frying pan on the stove and turn on the heat to **medium-low.** Push the butter around with a wooden spoon until it is all melted.

4

Measure 2 teaspoons **dried mint.** Sprinkle the mint into the butter. Mix it around in the butter for about 1 minute.

5

Add the peas, and sprinkle in a few shakes of **salt.** Stir gently with a wooden spoon.

Be careful not to smash the peas.

Let it cook for 5 minutes.

6

Meanwhile, tightly pile up 10 **fresh mint leaves** and snip them into tiny pieces with a scissors. Sprinkle them into the peas.

7

Stir gently, and use a fork to take a little taste. **Be careful not to burn your mouth!**

If you'd like it to be more buttery, you can add 1 more tablespoon butter and stir until it melts.

TIME TO EAT!

97

This wonderful dipping sauce for vegetables and tofu is both sweet and sour at the same time. It is incredibly yummy!

NOTE: Prepare the tofu and vegetables ahead of time, then put them on toothpicks for easy dipping.

INGREDIENTS:

- $1/2$ **cup water**
- **1 tablespoon soy sauce**
- **4 teaspoons cider vinegar**
- **4 teaspoons sugar or honey**
- $1/4$ **teaspoon salt**
- $1/2$ **teaspoon sesame oil**
- $1^1/2$ **teaspoons cornstarch**

FOR EXTRA FLAVOR (IF YOU CHOOSE):

- **1 teaspoon minced (cut in tiny pieces) or crushed garlic**
- **1 teaspoon peeled and grated fresh ginger**

THINGS TO DIP:

- **Little cubes of tofu**
- **Baby carrots, cooked or raw**
- **Cucumber slices**
- **Red bell pepper slices**
- **Pieces of cooked broccoli or other cooked vegetables**

YIELD: This recipe makes about $1/2$ cup of sauce—enough for about 4 people to dip lots of tasty tidbits.

TIME: It takes about 5 minutes to make and another 5 minutes to cook. (It takes a little longer to prepare if you add the garlic and ginger.)

YOU WILL ALSO NEED:

- 2-cup liquid measure
- Measuring spoons
- Whisk (a smaller one than usual, if you have one)
- Small, sharp knife and a cutting board (or garlic press), if adding the garlic
- Small handheld grater and a plate, if adding the ginger
- Small pot
- Small serving bowl
- Toothpicks and napkins or plates

ASK AN ADULT FOR HELP WITH:

- *Helping figure out when the sauce is ready*
- *Pouring the hot sauce into the serving bowl*

1

Put into a 2-cup measuring cup:

- ¹/₂ cup **water**
- 1 tablespoon **soy sauce**
- 4 teaspoons **vinegar**
- 4 teaspoons **sugar** or **honey**
- ¹/₄ teaspoon **salt**
- ¹/₂ teaspoon **sesame oil**

Whisk!

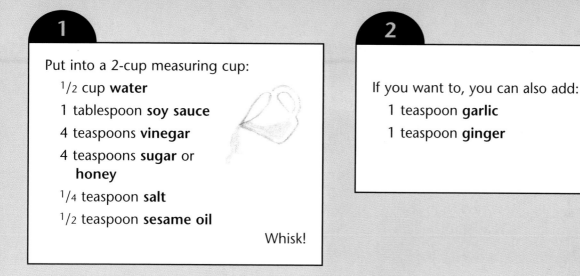

2

If you want to, you can also add:

- 1 teaspoon **garlic**
- 1 teaspoon **ginger**

3

Measure 1¹/₂ teaspoons **cornstarch** into a small pot. Slowly pour in the sauce and whisk until the cornstarch disappears.

4

Put the pot on the stove and turn on the heat to **medium**. Cook, whisking often, until it thickens a little. This will take about 2 or 3 minutes.

Ask an adult to help figure out when it's ready.

5

Ask an adult to help pour the hot sauce into a small serving bowl.

Put the bowl on the table.

6

Use a toothpick to dip pieces of tofu and vegetables in the delicious sauce.

TIME TO EAT!

In the days when there really was a Wild West, chili was a very important food for cowboys. They packed it up and carried it with them to eat while out on the range, riding their horses and driving cattle. Chili started out as a meat dish; spicy chiles were added to keep meat tasting fresh. But the cowboys also added beans to their chili so they could have more in the cooking pot. Eventually, chili became known in some places as a bean dish instead of a meat one.

This version has no meat. Instead, it is full of beans and vegetables. You can still think of it as real cowboy food, because it has seasonings in it (cumin and chile powder) to make it spunky like it was in the old days. It is a great dish to make in cold weather, when people are hungrier than usual and want something a little bit spicy to warm their toes.

There is some preparation to do ahead of time: chopping onions, carrots, peppers, and garlic, and grating cheese. You might want to ask for adult help, or maybe get an older sibling or a friend to pitch in. At serving time, choose from a selection of toppings: sour cream, grated cheese, or salsa. (You can make your own salsa, if you want to. The recipe is on page 154.) And don't forget to serve some tortilla chips on the side (try the homemade ones on page 146). They taste really good with this chili.

INGREDIENTS:

- 2 tablespoons olive oil
- 1 1/2 cups chopped onion
- 1 medium carrot, peeled and chopped or sliced
- 1 stalk celery, chopped
- 2 tablespoons mild chile powder
- 2 teaspoons ground cumin
- 3/4 teaspoon salt
- 1 tablespoon cider vinegar
- 1 small bell pepper, seeded and chopped
- 2 teaspoons minced (cut in tiny pieces) or crushed garlic
- 3 (15-ounce) cans red kidney beans, rinsed and drained (or about 5 cups cooked kidney beans)
- 2 cups tomato juice

TO SERVE ON OR WITH THE CHILI (YOU CHOOSE, AND USE AS MUCH AS YOU LIKE):

- Sour cream
- Grated cheddar cheese
- Salsa
- Tortilla chips

YIELD: This recipe makes 6 to 8 servings.

TIME: It takes about 1 hour, start to finish.

YOU WILL ALSO NEED:

- Small, sharp knife (and maybe a garlic press) and a cutting board for preparing the vegetables ahead of time
- Can opener
- Large wire-mesh strainer and a bowl it fits over for rinsing and draining the beans ahead of time
- Soup pot with a lid
- Measuring cups and spoons
- Long-handled wooden spoon
- 2-cup liquid measure
- Serving spoon or ladle
- Bowls and spoons or forks

ASK AN ADULT FOR HELP WITH:

- *Getting all of the vegetables cut and ready ahead of time*
- *Opening the cans of beans*
- *Rinsing and draining the beans*
- *Opening the cans of tomato juice*
- *Lifting the lid of the pot when it's time to stir (Hot steam will escape when the lid is lifted!)*
- *Ladling the hot chili into bowls*

1

Put a soup pot on the stove. Add 2 tablespoons **olive oil.**

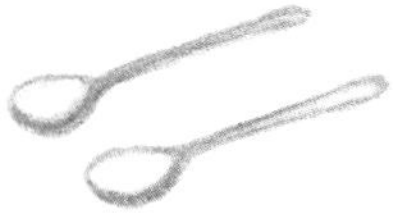

2

Turn on the heat to **medium,** and wait for 30 seconds.

3

Put in the pot:
  1 1/2 cups **onion**
  the **carrot**
  the **celery**
  2 tablespoons **chile powder**
  2 teaspoons **cumin**
  3/4 teaspoon **salt**

4

Cook the vegetables for 10 minutes, stirring every few minutes with a wooden spoon.

5

Add:
  1 tablespoon **cider vinegar**
  the **bell pepper**
  2 teaspoons **garlic**
  the **beans**

Stir, and cook for 5 minutes.

6

Measure 2 cups **tomato juice.** Pour it in slowly.

7

Stir gently, cover, and turn the heat to **low.** Cook for 20 minutes, stirring about every 5 minutes.

Ask an adult to lift the lid when it's time to stir, then to put it back on.

8

Ask an adult to help ladle or spoon the hot chili into bowls.

Serve with the toppings of your choice, and maybe also with tortilla chips on the side.

TIME TO EAT!

CHAPTER 4

DESSERTS AND A FEW BAKED THINGS

Basic Yeasted Dough and **Dinner Rolls**

Dough is so much fun! You can move it around and make it into shapes. You can also wrap it around fillings to make pastries. This dough can be used to make many things—as you'll see in the following pages.

Give yourself a lot of time because the dough needs 1 hour to rise. (That means you leave it sitting in its bowl while the yeast makes it gets bigger.) Find something to do while you're waiting.

A NOTE ABOUT YEAST: Yeast is a powdery ingredient that "wakes up" when it is dissolved in water and, once it is added to dough, makes the dough puff up and grow to nearly twice its size! The yeast only works when the water it is dissolved in isn't too hot. Check to be sure the water is the same temperature as you. (Do a little test by sticking a pinky into the water. It should feel neither hot nor cold but just slightly warm.)

INGREDIENTS:

- 1¹/4 cups lukewarm water
- 1 teaspoon active dry yeast
- 1 tablespoon sugar
- 2 tablespoons butter
- 3 cups pastry flour, plus extra for handling the dough
- 1¹/4 teaspoons salt

YIELD: *Half* of this recipe makes 8 Dinner Rolls, 16 Honest Pretzels, 4 Apple Pockets, or 6 Cinnamon Swirl Sticky Buns.

TIME: It takes about 10 minutes to make the dough and 1 hour to rest the dough.

YOU WILL ALSO NEED:

- 2-cup liquid measure
- Measuring cups and spoons
- Dinner knife for cutting butter
- Small bowl or pot for melting butter
- Medium-sized bowl
- Brush for painting butter
- Food processor fitted with the steel blade
- Table with board or countertop ("work area")
- Clean kitchen towel
- Scissors or a pastry cutter
- 1-gallon sealable freezer bag

ASK AN ADULT FOR HELP WITH:

- *Taking the melted butter out of the microwave or off the stove*
- *Measuring 1 tablespoon of the melted butter and putting it into the water-yeast mixture*
- *Setting up the food processor and taking the dough out of it*
- *Dividing and storing the dough until it's time to use it*

NOTES TO THE ADULT:

ABOUT STORING AND FREEZING THE DOUGH:
Basic Yeasted Dough freezes beautifully if stored in a sealed plastic freezer bag. Since this recipe makes double the dough you'll need for the recipes on pages 108–119, you may want to freeze the unused half for your next project. Defrost the frozen dough for at least 4 hours in the refrigerator—or 2 hours at room temperature—before using. You can freeze the dough for up to a month.

IF YOU DON'T HAVE A FOOD PROCESSOR:
Ideally, the kids should make the dough themselves (with some adult help), using a food processor. But, if you don't have one, here is a method for making the dough by hand. Hand-mixing bread dough is difficult for a child, so you will have to do most of it, but children can do the measuring and kneading. The amounts are the same as listed.

Put the lukewarm water into a medium-sized mixing bowl. Sprinkle in the yeast, sugar, and salt, stir, and let it stand for 5 minutes. Stir in 1 tablespoon of the melted butter. Add 1 cup of the flour, and beat with a whisk. Gradually add the remaining flour, mixing first with a wooden spoon and then with floured hands, until the dough comes together. (It will be somewhat soft.) Add just enough additional flour to keep the dough from being very sticky. Turn out the dough onto a floured work area and knead for about 5 minutes. Wash and dry the bowl and add the other 1 tablespoon of melted butter to the clean bowl. Proceed with Step 11 of the recipe (bottom of page 107).

DINNER ROLLS
This recipe is on page 108.

INGREDIENTS:
- ¹/₂ recipe Basic Yeasted Dough
- Flour, as needed, for handling the dough
- 1 tablespoon butter

YIELD: This recipe makes 8 rolls.

TIME: After the Basic Yeasted Dough is made and has risen, it takes 1¹/₂ hours, start to finish to make the rolls.

YOU WILL ALSO NEED:
- Table with board or countertop ("work area")
- Scissors or a pastry cutter
- Dinner knife for cutting butter
- Small bowl or pot for melting butter
- Brush for painting the muffin cups with butter
- Muffin pan with 12 standard-sized cups
- Timer with a bell
- Plate

ASK AN ADULT FOR HELP WITH:
- *Taking the melted butter out of the microwave or off the stove*
- *Turning on the oven*
- *Putting the pan in the oven and taking it out*
- *Taking the rolls out of the pan*

1

Measure 1¹/4 cups **lukewarm water** in a 2-cup liquid measuring cup.

"Lukewarm" means that when you dip your clean pinky into the water, it should feel no warmer or cooler than your pinky. Let it cool down for a few minutes if it's too warm.

2

Measure 1 teaspoon **yeast** and 1 tablespoon **sugar,** and sprinkle both of these into the water.

3

Use a dinner knife to cut 2 tablespoons **butter.** Each line on the butter wrapper means 1 tablespoon.

4

Put the butter in a small bowl and heat it in the microwave for 30 seconds on **high** until it is melted. (Or melt it in a small pot on the stove over **low** heat.)

Ask an adult to take the butter out (or off the stove).

5

Ask an adult to measure out 1 tablespoon of the melted butter and put it in the cup of water.

Put the rest of the **melted butter** into a medium-sized bowl and brush it around.

Set the bowl aside.

6

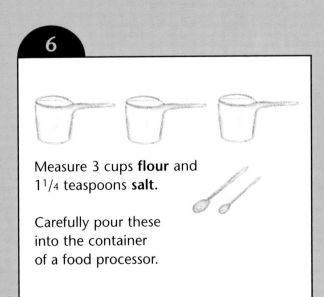

Measure 3 cups **flour** and 1¹/4 teaspoons **salt.**

Carefully pour these into the container of a food processor.

7

Turn on the food processor. As it runs, pour all of the **water mixture** in through the feed tube.

8

Keep the food processor running. In just a few seconds the water will have turned the flour into dough.

9

Leave the dough in the food processor for a minute while you sprinkle some extra flour onto the work area.

Also, rub some flour into the palms of your clean hands.

10

Ask an adult to take the dough out of the food processor and put it on the work area where you sprinkled the flour.

Push the dough together into a smooth ball, adding more flour to your hands if the dough feels sticky. Push it around and into itself for 2 or 3 minutes.

11

Put the ball of dough into the bowl with the butter in it. Swish the dough around, and then turn it upside-down and put it back in the bowl.

Cover the bowl with a clean kitchen towel and let the dough rest for 1 hour.

It will puff up a lot during this time.

12

After the dough has rested for 1 hour, use scissors or a pastry cutter to cut it in half.

Ask an adult to wrap one half of the dough in a plastic bag and put it in the refrigerator or freezer for later use.

The other half is now ready to use. Look through the following pages for inspiration.

TIME TO SHAPE AND BAKE!

DINNER ROLLS

1

You have already made a batch of **Basic Yeasted Dough.** (The recipe is on the past few pages.) You will use half a batch for this recipe.

2

Sprinkle a little **flour** on the work area and put the dough on the flour. Use scissors or a pastry cutter to cut the dough into 8 equal parts.

3

Cut each section into 3 equal parts.

Rub some flour into the palms of your hands and roll each part into a little ball.

When you're done, you should have 24 balls.

4

Use a dinner knife to cut 1 tablespoon **butter.** Each line on the butter wrapper means 1 tablespoon.

5

Put the butter in a small bowl and heat it in the microwave on **high** for 30 seconds until it is melted. (Or melt it in a small pot on the stove on **low** heat.)

Ask an adult to take the butter out (or off the stove).

6

Paint 8 muffin cups with the melted butter. Pour a little water into any extra, empty cups.

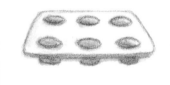

7

Put 3 balls of dough side by side in each muffin cup. When they are all in, let the dough sit for 30 minutes.

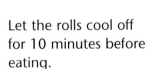

Meanwhile, **ask an adult to turn on the oven to 375°F.**

8

After 30 minutes, **ask an adult to put the pan in the oven.**

Set the timer for 15 minutes.

Ask an adult to take the pan out of the oven and the rolls out of the pan.

9

Let the rolls cool off for 10 minutes before eating.

TIME TO EAT!

HONEST PRETZELS

These handmade pretzels are way more interesting than the store-bought kind: They're chewy on the outside, and soft and tender on the inside—*and* you get to make them any shape you want! Honest Pretzels are especially good when eaten warm, soon after baking.

INGREDIENTS:

- ¹/₂ recipe Basic Yeasted Dough (page 104)
- Can of vegetable oil cooking spray or canola oil
- Flour, as needed, for handling the dough
- Water, for spritzing
- Salt, regular or kosher (optional)

YIELD: This recipe makes 16 pretzels.

TIME: After the Basic Yeasted Dough is made and has risen, these take about 1 hour, start to finish.

YOU WILL ALSO NEED:

- Large, wide pot for the water
- Brush for painting the baking tray with oil (if using oil)
- Baking tray
- Scissors or pastry cutter
- Table with board or countertop ("work area")
- A 12-inch ruler for measuring dough
- Slotted spoon
- Spray bottle filled with clean water
- Timer with a bell
- Spatula or tongs for handling the pretzels
- Plate

ASK AN ADULT FOR HELP WITH:

- *Filling the pot with water and putting it on the stove*
- *Heating the water*
- *Turning on the oven*
- *Putting the pretzels in and taking them out of the hot water*
- *Putting the tray in the oven*
- *Turning the pretzels over and spraying them during baking*
- *Taking the pretzels out of the oven and putting them on a plate to cool*

NOTE TO THE ADULT:

The water in the pot should be at least 3 inches deep. Bring it to a boil and then lower the heat so it is simmering very gently when you add the pretzels.

If you have any Pretzels left over, heat them in an oven or toaster oven right before eating so they'll taste fresh.

1

Have the dough ready.

Ask an adult to put on a pot of water to boil and to turn on the oven to 450°F.

Spray or brush a baking tray all over with a little **oil.**

2

Use scissors or a pastry cutter to cut the dough into 16 parts.

To get 16 parts, cut the dough into 4, then cut each piece into 4 again.

3

One at a time, roll or stretch each piece into a snake that is 12 inches (1 foot) long.

If the dough stiffens up, leave it alone for about 10 minutes, and then continue.

4

Shape the pretzels like this:

cross over   cross over again   fold down

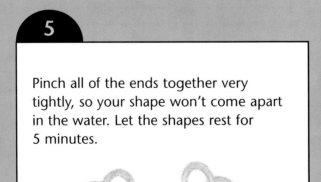

You can also make your snakes into bagel shapes or other shapes. They will taste the same.

5

Pinch all of the ends together very tightly, so your shape won't come apart in the water. Let the shapes rest for 5 minutes.

6

Ask an adult to put the shapes into the boiling water for 1 minute and then to take them out quickly with a slotted spoon and put them on the baking tray.

The pretzels will have to take turns going into the water. They cannot all fit at the same time.

7

Lightly spray the pretzels on the tray with **water**. 
This will make them crispy.

If you want to,
you can sprinkle them
with a little **salt**.

8

Ask an adult to put the tray in the oven.

Set the timer for 8 minutes.

8 1/2

Ask an adult to open the oven, turn the pretzels over, spray them with more water, and then close the oven again.

9

Set the timer for 7 minutes more.

Ask an adult to take the tray out of the oven and put the pretzels on a plate.

10

Wait 5 or 10 minutes to eat your pretzels, so you don't burn your mouth.

TIME
TO EAT!

111

Do you like apple pie? If so, you're going to love this.

This recipe is like individual apple pies made with a bread dough that gets very crispy in the oven. The reason it gets crispy is because you do something weird to it before you bake it: You actually spray it with water! The water, plus a little sugar that you sprinkle on top, gives it a wonderful crust.

"It's easy to cut apples when you've already—what's it called?—*cored* them."
—Tali

The first thing you do is make Basic Yeasted Dough (page 104). Plan ahead because the dough needs a whole hour to rise. While the dough is rising, you'll make a very simple filling of apples, cornstarch (to thicken the juices that come out of the apples as they bake), sugar, and cinnamon. Then you wrap the filling in circles of dough and bake until crisp.

You can eat these warm if you want to, or maybe even with a little vanilla ice cream on the side. Yummmm!

Another possibility: You can put these together in the evening, put the unbaked Apple Pockets on the baking tray, cover it tightly, and store it in the refrigerator overnight. In the morning, your parents can turn on the oven for you and you can unwrap the tray and put it right into the oven. This way you can have warm Apple Pockets for breakfast!

INGREDIENTS:

- $^1/_2$ recipe Basic Yeasted Dough (page 104)
- Vegetable oil cooking spray or a little soft butter for the baking tray
- $1^1/_2$ teaspoons cornstarch
- 7 teaspoons sugar
- $^1/_4$ teaspoon cinnamon
- 2 large tart apples, red or green (1 pound total)
- Flour, as needed, for handling the dough
- 1 tablespoon butter
- Water, for spritzing

YIELD: This makes 4 Apple Pockets (big enough to share).

TIME: After the Basic Yeasted Dough is made and has risen, the pastries take about 30 minutes to make, 25 minutes to bake, and 15 minutes to cool. That's about 1 hour and 10 minutes, start to finish.

"When you are rolling dough, flour is your friend." —Mo

YOU WILL ALSO NEED:

- Baking tray
- Waxed paper or a paper towel for buttering the tray (if using butter)
- Small bowl
- Measuring spoons
- Small spoon
- Vegetable peeler
- Small, sharp knife and a cutting board
- Medium-sized bowl
- Wooden spoon
- Table with board or countertop ("work area")
- Scissors or a pastry cutter
- Rolling pin
- A 12-inch ruler for measuring dough
- Dinner knife for cutting butter
- Small bowl or pot for melting butter
- Brush for painting melted butter
- Fork to press pocket edges closed
- Spray bottle filled with clean water
- Timer with a bell
- Plates

ASK AN ADULT FOR HELP WITH:

- *Turning on the oven*
- *Cutting out the apple cores*
- *Taking the melted butter out of the microwave or off the stove*
- *Putting the tray into the oven, taking it out, and putting the Apple Pockets on a plate*

1

Have the **dough** ready.

Ask an adult to turn on the oven to 400°F.

Spray a baking tray with **oil** or rub it all over with a little soft **butter** using waxed paper or a paper towel.

2

Put into a small bowl:

$1^1/_2$ teaspoons **cornstarch**

5 teaspoons of the **sugar**

$^1/_4$ teaspoon **cinnamon**

Mix well with a small spoon until it is all one color.

3

Peel 2 **apples** with a vegetable peeler and then cut the peeled apples into quarters on the cutting board.

Ask an adult to cut out the seed area (core) of each quarter.

Cut the apples into thin slices and put them in a medium-sized bowl.

4

Sprinkle the cornstarch mixture into the bowl of apple slices and mix gently with a wooden spoon until the apples are completely coated.

Set this aside for now.

5

Sprinkle a little **flour** onto the work area.

Put the dough on the flour and use a scissors or a pastry cutter to cut the dough into 4 equal parts.

Using clean hands, form each part into a ball. Put a little flour on your hands if the dough feels sticky.

6

Rub some flour on a rolling pin. Roll each ball of dough into a circle 6 or 7 inches wide.

Roll in all directions to make it round. Let the dough rest for a few minutes if it stiffens up.

7

Use a dinner knife to cut 1 tablespoon butter. Each line on the butter wrapper means 1 tablespoon.

8

Put the butter in a small bowl and heat it in the microwave on **high** for 30 seconds, until melted (or melt it in a small pot on the stove over **low** heat).

Ask an adult to take the butter out (or off the stove).

9

Brush some of the **melted butter** onto each circle of dough. Divide the apples into 4 parts and put 1 part onto one side of each of the 4 circles. Leave an edge.

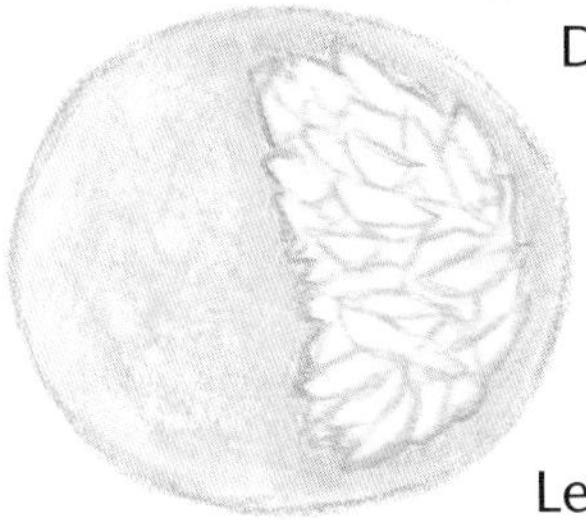

10

Fold over the other side of the circle to make it look like this shape.

Press the edges tightly closed with the back of a fork.

11

Put the pockets on the baking tray. Lightly spray them with **water**, and then sprinkle the top of each one with $1/2$ teaspoon sugar.

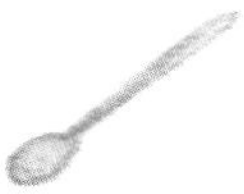

12

Ask an adult to put the tray in the oven.

Set the timer for 25 minutes.

Ask an adult to take out the tray and put the Apple Pockets on a plate to cool.

Wait 15 minutes before serving.

TIME TO EAT!

Cinnamon Swirl Sticky Buns

After you try this recipe, you might decide to go out and get a job in a real bakery. You will be that experienced!

Cinnamon Swirl Sticky Buns are made from Basic Yeasted Dough (page 104) that is stretched into an oval shape, sprinkled with cinnamon-sugar, and then rolled up tightly into a log. When you slice the log into pieces, there is a pretty swirl pattern inside. You bake the buns in a lot of butter with cinnamon and brown sugar, all of which creates a sweet and sticky coating that frosts the buns.

These buns make a great snack or dessert. You can also make them for a weekend breakfast. But since you and your parents probably don't want to get up at

5 o'clock in the morning even to make *these,* here is what to do. Make the dough and put the buns together and into the muffin pan the night before. Cover the pan tightly with plastic wrap, and refrigerate it overnight. In the morning, ask your parents to turn on the oven. Take the pan out of the refrigerator, uncover it, and put it right into the preheated oven. About 25 minutes later, these delicious sticky buns will be done. Let them cool off a little, then dig in.

INGREDIENTS:

- ¹/₂ recipe Basic Yeasted Dough (page 104)
- Flour, as needed, for handling the dough
- 2 tablespoons white sugar
- 2 teaspoons cinnamon
- 5 tablespoons butter
- 2 tablespoons brown sugar

YIELD: This recipe makes 6 buns.

TIME: After the Basic Yeasted Dough is made and has risen, these take 30 minutes to make, 45 minutes to rest, and 40 minutes to bake and cool. That's about 2 hours, start to finish.

YOU WILL ALSO NEED:

- Table with board or countertop ("work area")
- Scissors or pastry cutter
- Measuring spoons
- Small bowl and spoon for mixing cinnamon-sugar
- Possibly a rolling pin
- Dinner knife for cutting butter
- Small bowl or pot for melting butter
- Brush for painting melted butter
- Dinner knife or pastry cutter for slicing rolled-up dough
- Muffin pan with 6 standard-sized cups
- Timer with a bell
- Plate

ASK AN ADULT FOR HELP WITH:

- *Taking the butter out of the microwave or off the stove*
- *Turning on the oven*
- *Putting the pan in the oven and taking it out*
- *Taking the sticky buns out of the pan and putting them upside-down on a plate*

"Stand the sticky buns on their hind legs in the muffin pan, and push them in with your fingers." —Emily

1

Have the **dough** ready.

Lightly sprinkle the work area with **flour** and then put the dough on the flour.

2

Meanwhile, put into a small bowl:

2 tablespoons **white sugar**

2 teaspoons **cinnamon**

Mix until it is all one color. Set this aside.

3

Back to the dough. Rub some flour on your clean palms or on a rolling pin. *Slowly* stretch or roll each piece of dough into a rectangle or oval about 12 inches long and 6 inches wide.

If the dough stiffens up, let it rest for about 10 minutes, then continue.

4

Use a dinner knife to cut 5 tablespoons of the **butter.** Each line on the butter wrapper means 1 tablespoon.

5

Put the butter in a small bowl and heat it in the microwave on **high** for 1 minute, until it is melted. (Or melt it in a small pot on the stove over **low** heat.)

Ask an adult to take the butter out (or off the stove).

6

Brush the stretched-out dough all over with half the **melted butter.**

Brush 6 muffin cups with the rest of the butter and set the pan aside for now.

7

Sprinkle half of the **cinnamon-sugar mixture** on the buttered area of the dough.

Save the other half of the cinnamon-sugar.

8

Roll up the dough this way:

It will look like a log. Using your thumb and forefinger, pinch the edges tightly closed.

9

Use a dinner knife or a pastry cutter to slice the log into 6 similar pieces.
They don't have to be *exactly* equal.

10

Remember the other half of the cinnamon-sugar? Add 2 tablespoons **brown sugar** to it and crumble it all together with your clean fingers.

11

Sprinkle this mixture as evenly as possible into the buttery muffin cups.

Put the buns in the muffin cups, with the cut sides facing up.

Pinch the tops together to close them up so the filling doesn't show.

Let them rest for 45 minutes.

12

While the buns are resting, ask an adult to turn on the oven to 375°F.

12¹/₂

After the buns have rested, ask an adult to put the pan in the oven.

Set the timer for 25 minutes.

Ask an adult to take them out.

13

Ask an adult to lift out the buns with a fork and put them upside-down on a plate.

Cool for 15 minutes before eating.

TIME TO EAT!

PEANUT BUTTER DOO-DADS

Here's a fun recipe that uses just three ingredients: peanut butter, chocolate chips, and cereal (Cheerios, Rice Krispies, or Grape Nuts). You get to choose which kind of cereal to use. And remember, you can make these more than once and choose a different kind each time!

These are not exactly cookies, and they're not really candy, either. They're something in between, which is why I call them "Doo-Dads." They taste good enough to be dessert, but they are just healthy enough that your parents probably won't mind if you have them as an after-school snack. (Ask them.)

Be sure to use a high-quality peanut butter for this—the kind made from peanuts without a lot of other stuff added. You can use either crunchy or smooth. (Or, make your own peanut butter with the recipe on page 52.) Peanut Butter Doo-Dads will keep for weeks in the refrigerator or freezer if stored in a tightly closed container.

INGREDIENTS:

- 1/2 cup high-quality peanut butter
- 1/3 cup semisweet chocolate chips
- 1 cup cereal (Cheerios, Rice Krispies, or Grape Nuts)

YIELD: This recipe makes about 30 Doo-Dads, depending on the size.

TIME: It takes about 20 minutes to make and 1 hour to chill (or 15 minutes to freeze). That's 1 hour and 20 minutes (or 35 minutes), start to finish.

YOU WILL ALSO NEED:

- Soup spoon for scooping peanut butter
- Measuring cups
- Frying pan
- Rubber spatula
- Wooden spoon
- Cutting board or kitchen towel
- 2 soup spoons or teaspoons for scooping batter
- Several regular or very large plates

ASK AN ADULT FOR HELP WITH:

- ***Handling the peanut butter***
- ***Handling the hot pan***

1

Measure 1/2 cup **peanut butter**. Put it into a frying pan.

Ask an adult to help you scrape it all in with a rubber spatula.

2

Put the pan on the stove and turn on the heat to **medium**.

Stir with a wooden spoon for about 1 minute, or until the peanut butter is very soft. Take the pan off the stove and put it on a board or a kitchen towel. **You might need an adult to help.**

3

Measure 1/3 cup **chocolate chips** and dump them in. Stir until they are soft and a little melted.

4

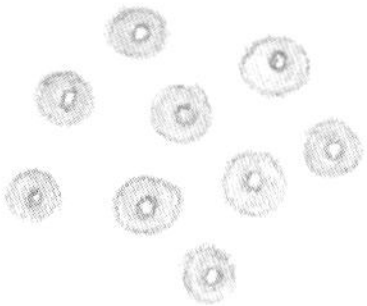

Measure 1 cup **cereal** and dump it in.

5

Mix slowly until the cereal is all coated and gooey.

6

Scoop up a spoonful of the stuff. Use another spoon to push it from the spoon onto a large plate. It will look like a brown lump. Do this with all of the batter.

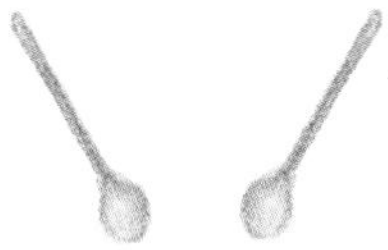

7

When you have finished making all of the batter into lumps, put the plate, uncovered, in the refrigerator for at least 1 hour. The lumps (Doo-Dads) will get firm.

For faster results, put them in the freezer. They'll be ready in 15 minutes!

TIME TO EAT!

If you are looking for an unusual treat to bring to class on your birthday, try these cupcakes. (You can make them on an ordinary day, too!) They are vanilla cupcakes with a big chocolate dot in the middle, like a giant button. The button is really a Hershey's Kiss, which you push into the batter with your finger. It looks so neat, you won't need to frost or decorate the cupcakes after they are baked.

In addition to being special and unusual, this recipe is quite easy. The only tricky part is spooning the batter into the muffin cups. (It's not difficult to do, just a little messy. Ask an adult to help you with this part, and take your time.)

If you have an eager younger sibling hanging around who needs a job, consider letting him or her put the muffin papers in the pan.

BONUS SITUATION: If you buy a whole bag of Hershey's Kisses to use for this recipe, you'll have a lot of them left over. Hope you can figure out something to do with them.

INGREDIENTS:

- 1 1/2 cups unbleached white flour
- 1/2 teaspoon salt
- 1 1/2 teaspoons baking powder
- 3/4 cup sugar
- 1/2 cup milk
- 2 eggs
- 1 teaspoon vanilla extract
- 1 stick butter
- 12 Hershey's Kisses

YIELD: This recipe makes 12 cupcakes.

TIME: It takes about 20 minutes to make, 20 minutes to bake, and 15 minutes to cool. That's just about 1 hour, start to finish.

YOU WILL ALSO NEED:

- Muffin papers
- Muffin pan with 12 standard-sized cups
- Medium-sized wire-mesh strainer plus a bowl it fits over
- Measuring cups and spoons
- Wooden spoon
- 2-cup liquid measure
- Small bowl for the eggs
- Small bowl or pot for melting butter
- Whisk
- Handheld electric mixer
- Rubber spatula
- Soup spoon for spooning batter
- Timer with a bell

ASK AN ADULT FOR HELP WITH:

- *Turning on the oven*
- *Taking the melted butter out of the microwave or off the stove*
- *Setting up and using the electric mixer*
- *Helping you spoon the batter into the muffin cups*
- *Putting the pan into the oven and taking it out*
- *Taking the cupcakes out of the pan to cool*

"This stuff makes a *very* special dessert.
You could have it for your birthday"
—Susie

1

Ask an adult to turn on the oven to 350°F.

Put muffin papers in a muffin pan with 12 muffin cups.

2

Put a strainer over a bowl. Put in the strainer:

  1 1/2 cups **flour**
  1/2 teaspoon **salt**
  1 1/2 teaspoons **baking powder**

Gently shake the strainer up and down until everything sifts into the bowl.

3

Add 3/4 cup **sugar.** Stir with a wooden spoon to mix in the sugar, and make a dent in the center. Put this aside for now.

4

Pour the **milk** into a 2-cup measuring cup until it reaches the line for 1/2 cup.

5

Break 2 **eggs** into a bowl. Add these to the milk, along with 1 teaspoon **vanilla extract.**

6

Put a whole stick of **butter** into a bowl, and heat it in the microwave on **high** for 1 1/2 minutes, until it is melted. (Or melt it in a pot on the stove over **low** heat.)

Ask an adult to take the butter out (or off the stove) and pour it into the milk mixture.

7

Slowly whisk the **milk mixture** until it is all one color and you don't see any egg yolk.

Carefully pour this into the dent in the **flour mixture**.

8

Ask an adult for help with steps 8 and 9.

Beat the batter with an electric mixer on **low** speed for 2 minutes.

Stop the mixer and put it down.

Pick up a rubber spatula and scrape the sides and bottom of the bowl a few times.

9

Beat again with the electric mixer, this time on **medium** speed. Do this for about 2 more minutes.

Put down the mixer and scrape the bowl again with the rubber spatula.

10

Put 2 full soup spoons of batter into each muffin paper. **This is messy. Ask for adult help if you need it.**

11

Put a **chocolate Kiss,** pointing down, into the center of each raw cupcake. Push it a little with your finger, like you're gently pushing a button. It should still show.

12

Ask an adult to put the pan in the oven. Set the timer for 20 minutes.

Ask an adult to take it out of the oven and to take the cupcakes out of the pan. Cool for 15 minutes before eating.

TIME TO EAT!

GREEN MINT CRINKLES

Sounds good. But what are they?

Crinkles are little round cookies that you make by rolling dough into small balls with your hands. They get a crinkly texture from a special ingredient—green crystals—the kind you use to decorate cakes and holiday cookies. You get to put a whole jar of this magical stuff right into the batter!

Peppermint extract is another unusual ingredient in this recipe. It smells really strong if you sniff it right from the bottle. But once it is in the batter it gives the cookies a very good and refreshing flavor.

Try these any time of year, but especially at holiday time, in December. They are incredibly cheerful!

INGREDIENTS:

- Can of vegetable oil cooking spray or a little soft butter for the baking tray
- 1 stick butter
- $3/4$ cup sugar
- 2 teaspoons peppermint extract
- 1 teaspoon vanilla extract
- 1 egg
- $1/4$ cup milk
- 2 cups unbleached white flour plus a little extra for handling the dough
- 2 teaspoons baking powder
- $1/4$ teaspoon salt
- 1 ($2 1/4$-ounce) jar green cake decoration crystals

YIELD: This recipe makes about $2 1/2$ dozen little cookies.

TIME: It takes 15 minutes to make and 12 minutes to bake, plus 10 minutes to cool. That's about 40 minutes, start to finish.

YOU WILL ALSO NEED:

- Waxed paper or a paper towel to butter the tray if using butter
- Baking tray
- Small bowl or pot for melting butter
- Rubber spatula
- Large mixing bowl
- Measuring cups and spoons
- Long-handled wooden spoon
- Small bowl and a fork for the egg
- 1-cup liquid measure
- Timer with a bell
- Spatula
- Plate

ASK AN ADULT FOR HELP WITH:

- *Turning on the oven*
- *Taking the melted butter out of the microwave (or off the stove) and scraping it into the mixing bowl*
- *Putting the tray into the oven and taking it out*
- *Putting the hot cookies on a plate to cool*

1

Ask an adult to turn on the oven to 350°F.

Spray a baking tray with **oil** or rub it all over with a little soft **butter** using waxed paper or a paper towel.

2

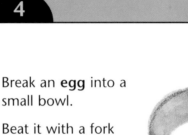

Put a whole stick of butter in a bowl and heat it in the microwave on **high** for 2 minutes, until it is melted. (Or melt it in a pot on the stove over **low** heat.)

Ask an adult to take it out (or off the stove) and scrape it into a large bowl.

3

Add to the butter in the bowl:
- 3/4 cup **sugar**
- 2 teaspoons **peppermint extract**
- 1 teaspoon **vanilla extract**

Mix together with a wooden spoon.

4

Break an **egg** into a small bowl.

Beat it with a fork until it is completely yellow and smooth.

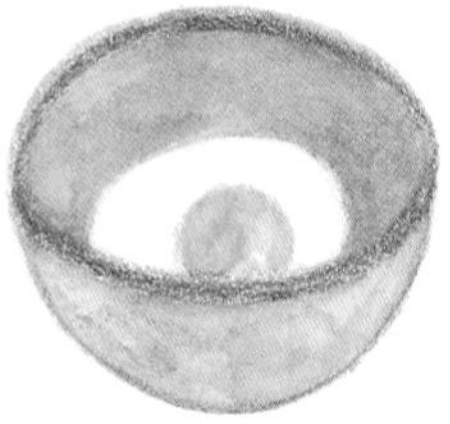

5

Pour the **milk** into the measuring cup until it reaches the line for 1/4 cup.

6

Add the egg and milk to the **butter-sugar mixture** and beat strongly, but not fast, with the wooden spoon until everything is all mixed in.

7

Add:

  2 cups **flour**
  2 teaspoons **baking powder**
  ¹/₄ teaspoon **salt**
  1 jar **green crystals**

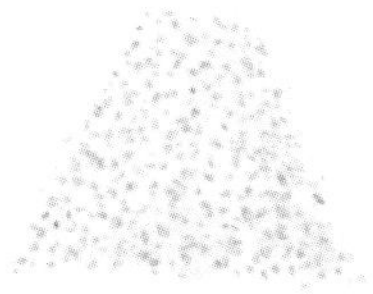

8

Mix strongly and slowly for a few minutes with the wooden spoon.

If it gets too thick to use the spoon, rub some flour on your clean palms and mix the batter with your clean hands until the flour and the green crystals are all blended in.

9

Rub some more flour on your palms.

Pick up little pieces of dough and roll them into balls the size of ping-pong balls (1 inch across).

10

Put all of the balls on the baking tray.
They can be close together but should not touch.

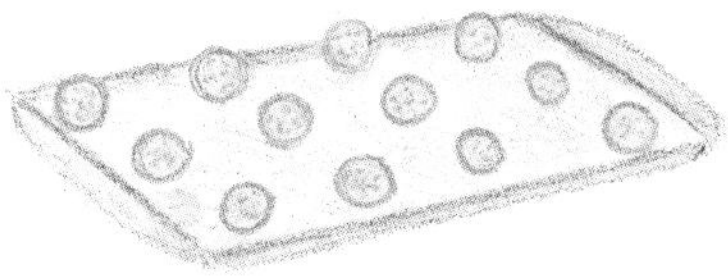

11

Ask an adult to put the tray in the oven.

Set the timer for 12 minutes.

12

Ask an adult to take it out of the oven and to put the cookies on a plate to cool.

Wait for 10 minutes before eating.

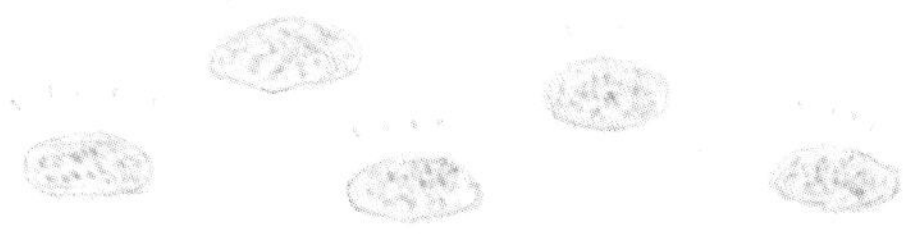

TIME TO EAT!

This must sound very strange. You don't use any bowls at all to make this cake—you just put everything right into the baking pan and stir it up. It looks like a mess! But go ahead and put it in the oven anyway, and say to yourself, "I believe." Because a real chocolate cake will come out of that oven, and you will feel like you just performed a miracle. If that isn't remarkable enough, this chocolate cake just *happens* to be one of the best ever—dark, moist, and tender. It is so good, in fact, that it doesn't even need any frosting. Just eat it plain, or with a little powdered sugar on top, and wash it down with a big glass of ice-cold milk. Terrific!

NOTE: This chocolate cake is 100 percent vegan. (Vegans are vegetarians who don't eat any eggs or dairy products.) So, if you are a vegan, wash it down with a big glass of ice-cold soy milk instead.

INGREDIENTS:
- 1¼ cups unbleached white flour
- ⅓ cup unsweetened cocoa
- 1 cup sugar
- ½ teaspoon salt
- ¾ teaspoon baking soda
- 1 cup water
- ⅓ cup canola or vegetable oil
- 1 teaspoon vanilla extract
- 1 teaspoon cider vinegar or white vinegar

YIELD: This recipe makes one 8-inch square cake, about 8 or 9 servings.

TIME: It takes about 15 minutes to make, 30 minutes to bake, and about 30 minutes to cool. That's 1 hour and 15 minutes, start to finish.

YOU WILL ALSO NEED:

- 8-inch square glass baking pan
- Measuring cups and spoons
- Fork and soup spoon for mixing
- 1-cup liquid measure
- Rubber spatula
- Damp paper towels
- Timer with a bell
- Knife and spatula for serving
- Plates and forks

ASK AN ADULT FOR HELP WITH:

- *Turning on the oven*
- *Helping you clean off the edges of the pan*
- *Putting the pan into the oven and taking it out*

ABSOLUTELY MARVELOUS!

1

Ask an adult to turn on the oven to 325°F.

2

Put into a square glass baking pan:

1^1/$_4$ cups **flour**

^{1}/$_3$ cup **cocoa**

1 cup **sugar**

^{1}/$_2$ teaspoon **salt**

^{3}/$_4$ teaspoon **baking soda**

3

Mix it slowly, taking turns with a fork and a soup spoon, until it is completely light brown. (You shouldn't see any more white. Peek through the bottom of the pan to be sure.)

4

When it is all mixed, make 4 dents with a spoon—2 large and 2 small—in the mixture.

5

Measure 1 cup **water** and pour it into one of the large dents.

6

Measure ^{1}/$_3$ cup **oil** and pour it into the other large dent.

7

Measure 1 teaspoon **vanilla extract** and pour it into one of the small dents.

8

Measure 1 teaspoon **vinegar** and pour it into the other small dent.

9

Begin stirring slowly with a fork in little circles to get all of the dry parts wet.

10

As it turns into batter, start mashing it down with the fork. After you mash a few times, scrape the bottom and stir.

Do this again many times: mash, scrape, and stir. Take your time.

11

When the batter is smooth, scrape the sides one more time with a rubber spatula and spread it into place.

Ask an adult to help you clean off the edges of the pan with a damp paper towel.

12

Ask an adult to put the pan in the oven.

Set the timer for 30 minutes.

Ask an adult to take it out.

13

Cool the cake in the pan for 30 minutes before cutting it into squares and taking each piece out with a spatula.

TIME TO EAT!

Banana bread is like a cross between a bread and a dessert. You can use this recipe for either. If you'd like it to be a bread, make it plain, and spread it with cream cheese or peanut butter for lunch or a snack. If you'd like it to be dessert, you can add chocolate chips and/or chopped nuts to the batter.

This is a perfect recipe to make as a gift for a special teacher or relative for a birthday or during the holiday season. You can wrap the whole loaf in colored foil and ribbons, or you can give someone a few thick slices on a pretty paper plate, wrap it in plastic wrap decorated with stickers. The lucky person you give this to will really appreciate receiving a gift you made yourself—especially this! (Ask your parents if you can make two loaves—one to keep and one to give away.)

The first step of this recipe—mashing very ripe bananas in a big bowl with a fork—is a whole lot of fun. If you have a younger sibling who would like to "help," this is a good job to let him or her do.

NOTE: Unwrap the stick of butter and put it in the mixing bowl an hour or two ahead of time so it can soften.

INGREDIENTS:
- 3 medium-sized very ripe bananas
- 3/4 cup plain yogurt
- 1 tablespoon butter for the pan
- 1 stick butter for the batter
- 3/4 cup brown sugar
- 1 teaspoon vanilla extract
- 2 eggs
- 2 1/2 cups unbleached white flour
- 1/2 teaspoon salt
- 1 1/2 teaspoons baking powder
- 1/2 teaspoon baking soda

EXTRAS (YOU CHOOSE):
- 1 cup semisweet chocolate chips
- 3/4 cup chopped walnuts, almonds, or pecans

YIELD: This recipe makes 1 large loaf.

TIME: It takes about 40 minutes to make, 1 hour to bake, and 30 minutes to cool. That's 2 hours and 10 minutes, start to finish.

YOU WILL ALSO NEED:

- Medium-sized bowl and a fork for mashing bananas
- Measuring cups and spoons
- Whisk
- Dinner knife for cutting butter and testing if bread is done
- Small bowl or pot for melting butter
- Standard-sized loaf pan
- Brush for painting the pan with butter
- Large mixing bowl
- Handheld electric mixer
- Small bowl and a fork for beating the eggs
- Rubber spatula
- Medium-sized wire-mesh strainer plus a bowl it fits over
- Long-handled wooden spoon
- Timer with a bell

ASK AN ADULT FOR HELP WITH:

- *Turning on the oven*
- *Taking the melted butter out of the microwave or off the stove*
- *Setting up and using the electric mixer*
- *Putting the pan in the oven*
- *Checking to see if the bread is done*
- *Taking the pan out of the oven*
- *Taking the bread out of the pan*

"They still smell like bananas, even when they're smashed." —Megan

135

1

Two hours ahead of time, unwrap a stick of **butter** and put it in a mixing bowl to soften.

When you're ready to start, **ask an adult to turn on the oven to 350°F.**

2

Peel 3 **bananas** and put them in a medium-sized bowl. Mash the bananas with a fork until they are totally mushy.

Add 3/4 cup **yogurt** and mix it in with a whisk. Put this aside for now.

3

Use a dinner knife to cut 1 tablespoon butter from another stick. Each line on the butter wrapper means 1 tablespoon.

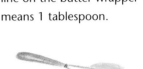

4

Put the butter in a small bowl and heat it in the microwave on **high** for 30 seconds. (Or melt it in a small pot on the stove over **low** heat.)

Ask an adult to take the butter out (or off the stove). Use a brush to paint **melted butter** all over the inside of a loaf pan.

5

You have a stick of soft butter already in a a big bowl, right?

Measure 3/4 cup **brown sugar** and crumble it into the butter using your clean fingers.

Add 1 teaspoon **vanilla extract.**

6

You might need an adult to help with steps 6 and 7.

Beat with an electric mixer on **high** speed for 2 minutes.

7

Break 2 **eggs** into a small bowl. Beat them lightly with a fork and then pour them into the big bowl.

Beat with an electric mixer on **medium** speed for 2 minutes.

Stop the mixer, scrape the sides and bottom of the bowl with a rubber spatula, and beat for 1 minute more.

8

Put a strainer over a medium-sized bowl. Put into the strainer:

- 2^1/$_2$ cups **flour**
- ^{1}/$_2$ teaspoon **salt**
- 1^1/$_2$ teaspoons **baking powder**
- ^{1}/$_2$ teaspoon **baking soda**

Gently shake the strainer up and down until everything sifts into the bowl.

9

Use a measuring cup with a handle to scoop up about half the **flour mixture** and put it into the **butter mixture**. Stir it in with a wooden spoon.

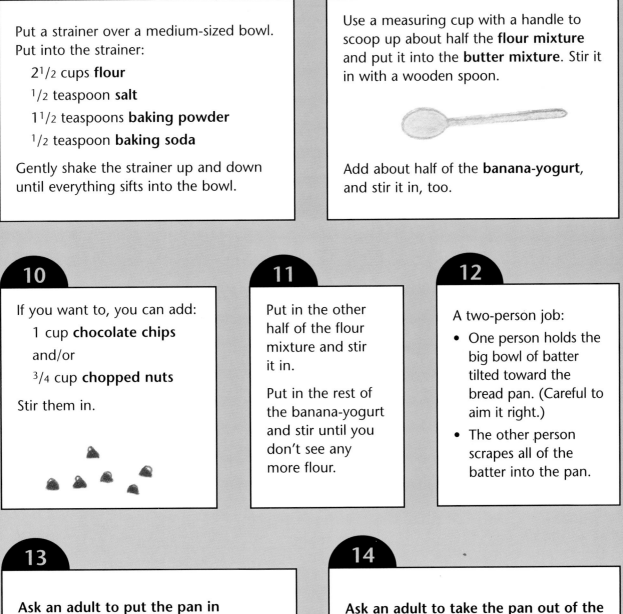

Add about half of the **banana-yogurt**, and stir it in, too.

10

If you want to, you can add:

- 1 cup **chocolate chips**
  and/or
- ^{3}/$_4$ cup **chopped nuts**

Stir them in.

11

Put in the other half of the flour mixture and stir it in.

Put in the rest of the banana-yogurt and stir until you don't see any more flour.

12

A two-person job:

- One person holds the big bowl of batter tilted toward the bread pan. (Careful to aim it right.)
- The other person scrapes all of the batter into the pan.

13

Ask an adult to put the pan in the oven.

Set the timer for 1 hour.

Ask an adult to check to see if it's done by sticking a knife all the way into the center. If it comes out clean, it's done. If not, the adult should put the bread back into the oven for 10 minutes.

14

Ask an adult to take the pan out of the oven and remove the bread from the pan. (Rap the pan sharply a few times; the bread should slide right out.)

Wait 30 minutes before slicing.

TIME TO EAT!

Raspberry Sauce

FOR A PLATTER OF FRUIT

Sometimes it's nice to have fruit for dessert. It's even nicer when you add a colorful touch of flavor to make it special.

Here is that special touch: a bright red sauce made from raspberries. You can make it any time of year—with fresh raspberries when they are in season, and with frozen unsweetened raspberries for all the other times.

You can serve this sauce on any kind of fruit. Try apples, pears, pineapple, kiwi, and bananas in the winter, and peaches, plums, grapes, and melon in the summer. Slice the fruit, then put it on a platter to make a lovely design. Whip up this sauce in the blender, strain out the crunchy seeds to make it smooth, and drizzle it on top. This also makes a wonderful breakfast dish—and a great topping for plain yogurt.)

If you want to, you can make the sauce ahead of time. It keeps for several days in the refrigerator in a tightly covered container.

INGREDIENTS:

- 1^1/$_2$ cups fresh raspberries (or 1^1/$_2$ cups frozen unsweetened berries, defrosted)
- 2 tablespoons sugar
- 3 tablespoons orange juice

YIELD: This recipe makes 1^1/$_2$ cups of sauce.

TIME: It takes 15 minutes, start to finish.

YOU WILL ALSO NEED:

- Measuring cups and spoons
- Blender
- Medium-sized wire-mesh strainer plus a bowl it fits over
- Rubber spatula
- Soup spoon
- Bowls or plates, forks or spoons

ASK AN ADULT FOR HELP WITH:

- *Setting up the blender and scraping all of the raspberry liquid out of it*
- *Slicing the fruit*

"Tearing this orange is fun. I don't even mind getting my hands wet." —Heather

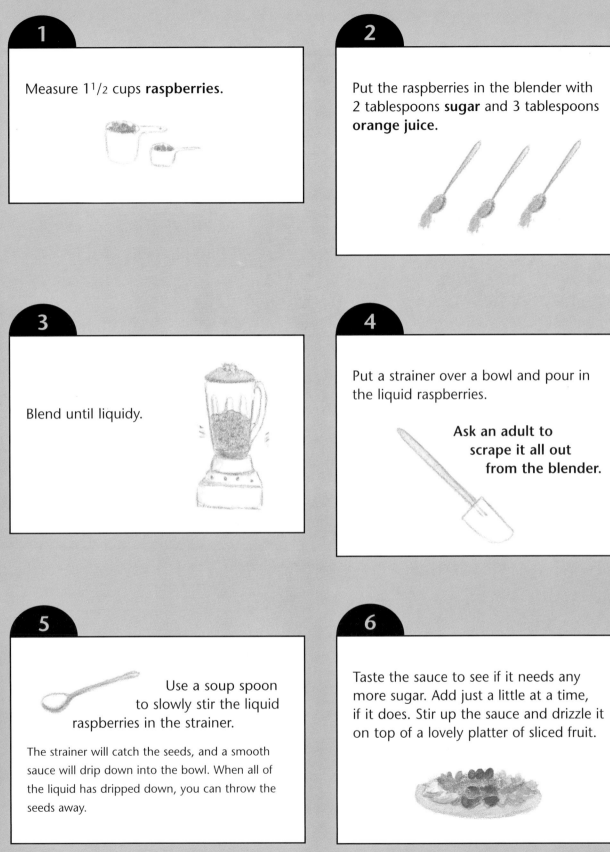

1

Measure 1 1/2 cups **raspberries.**

2

Put the raspberries in the blender with 2 tablespoons **sugar** and 3 tablespoons **orange juice.**

3

Blend until liquidy.

4

Put a strainer over a bowl and pour in the liquid raspberries.

Ask an adult to scrape it all out from the blender.

5

Use a soup spoon to slowly stir the liquid raspberries in the strainer.

The strainer will catch the seeds, and a smooth sauce will drip down into the bowl. When all of the liquid has dripped down, you can throw the seeds away.

6

Taste the sauce to see if it needs any more sugar. Add just a little at a time, if it does. Stir up the sauce and drizzle it on top of a lovely platter of sliced fruit.

TIME TO EAT!

139

Strawberry shortcake is usually made with a biscuit that is similar to the breakfast kind, only maybe a little sweeter. You split the biscuit open and put on some sliced strawberries. Then you top the whole thing with whipped cream.

This one is slightly different. Instead of regular biscuits, you bake a batch of yogurt scones, made with vanilla yogurt. Then, instead of putting on just strawberries, you use a mixture of berries—strawberries, blueberries, blackberries, raspberries. Use whatever you have. Different kinds of berries taste great together. This recipe is also special because we top the shortcake and berries with vanilla yogurt. It's delicious, and it's good for you, too.

INGREDIENTS:

- **Can of vegetable oil cooking spray or a little soft butter for the baking tray**
- **1 2/3 cups unbleached white flour plus a little extra for handling the dough**
- **1 teaspoon baking powder**
- **1 teaspoon baking soda**
- **1/4 teaspoon salt**
- **2/3 cup vanilla yogurt, plus extra for the topping**
- **1 egg**
- **1/2 stick (4 tablespoons) butter**
- **6 cups fresh berries (or frozen unsweetened berries, defrosted)**
- **4 tablespoons sugar, or more, to taste**

YIELD: This makes 6 generous servings.

TIME: It takes about 20 minutes to make, 15 minutes to bake, 30 minutes to cool, and about 5 minutes to assemble with the toppings. That's about 1 hour and 10 minutes, start to finish.

YOU WILL ALSO NEED:

- Waxed paper or a paper towel to butter the tray (if using butter)
- Baking tray
- Large wire-mesh strainer plus a bowl it fits over
- Measuring cups and spoons
- Soup spoon
- 2-cup liquid measure
- Small bowl for the egg
- Dinner knife for cutting the butter and shortcakes, and for scraping the spoon
- Small bowl or pot for melting butter
- Whisk
- Rubber spatula
- Long-handled wooden spoon
- Table with board or countertop ("work area")
- Pastry cutter or a dinner knife for cutting dough
- Medium-sized bowl for berries
- Fork for mixing berries
- Plates, forks, and spoons

ASK AN ADULT FOR HELP WITH:

- *Preparing the berries*
- *Turning on the oven*
- *Taking the melted butter out of the microwave (or off the stove) and scraping it into the liquid measure*
- *Putting the baking tray into the oven and taking it out*

NOTE TO THE ADULTS:

If the shortcake is made ahead and needs to be "refreshed," you can toast it lightly first.

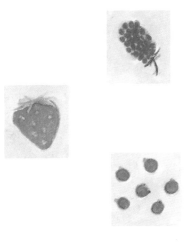

"This will be yummy!" —Shani

141

1

Ask an adult to turn on the oven to 400°F.

Spray a baking tray with **oil** or rub it all over with a little soft **butter,** using waxed paper or a paper towel.

2

Put a strainer over a bowl. Put into the strainer:

$1^2/_3$ cups **flour**

1 teaspoon **baking powder**

1 teaspoon **baking soda**

$^1/_4$ teaspoon **salt**

Gently shake the strainer up and down until everything sifts into the bowl. Put this aside for now.

3

Using a soup spoon, scoop the **yogurt** into a 2-cup measuring cup until it reaches the line for $^2/_3$ cup.

4

Break an **egg** into a small bowl and slide the egg into the yogurt in the cup.

5

Cut $^1/_2$ stick butter.

6

Melt it in a small bowl in the microwave on **high** for 1 minute (or in a small pot on the stove over **low** heat).

Ask an adult to take it out (or off the stove) and pour and scrape it into the yogurt and egg.

7

Whisk the mixture right in the measuring cup until it is one color and you don't see any more yolk.

8

Make a dent in the center of the **flour mixture** with a spoon.

Slowly pour in the **yogurt mixture**, scraping it all in with a rubber spatula.

9

Use a wooden spoon to mix strongly, but not quickly. The batter will be stiff, so you have to kind of mash it as you stir. Do this until it is all combined.

During the mixing, scrape off the spoon with a dinner knife or there will be more batter on the spoon than in the bowl!

10

Sprinkle some flour on the work surface and rub some flour into the palms of your clean hands.

11

Put the batter onto the work surface and pat and push it together in a flat ball, like a big biscuit.

12

Use a dinner knife or a pastry cutter to cut the batter into 6 equal pieces (like a "peace" sign with each section cut in half).

NOT TIME TO EAT YET! TURN THE PAGE...

13

Put the pieces on the baking tray.

Ask an adult to put it in the oven.

Set the timer for 15 minutes.

Ask an adult to take it out.

14

Let the cakes cool down for about 30 minutes. While they are cooling, prepare the **berries**.

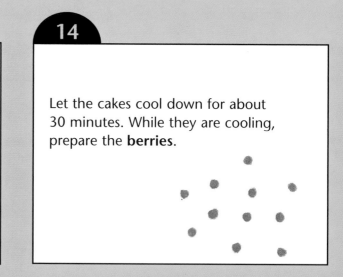

15

If you are using **strawberries**, pull off the stems, then slice the berries in half. (If they are huge, you can slice them in quarters.)

If you are using other kinds of berries, you don't have to do anything to them first.

16

Put all the berries in a bowl and sprinkle them with 4 tablespoons **sugar**.

Stir gently with a fork until all the sugar is mixed in.

Put this aside for now.

17

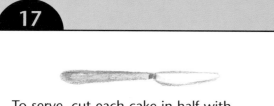

To serve, cut each cake in half with dinner knife so there is a top and a bottom, and put the 2 halves side-by-side on a plate.

18

Spoon on a lot of berries onto each half, and top with 2 big blobs of yogurt.

TIME TO EAT!

CHAPTER 5

SNACKS AND A FEW SPECIAL DRINKS

HOMEMADE Tortilla Chips

I don't know why, but when you make your own tortilla chips, they taste *soooo* much better than when you buy them in a store. (And the ones from the store taste pretty good to begin with.)

There are two very fun jobs in this recipe. One is cutting the tortillas into shapes with scissors. You can take your time doing this and really enjoy yourself.

The other fun part is spraying the tray and the cut tortillas with oil spray. When you do this, be sure you hold the can about 12 inches away from what you are spraying, and move the spray can around so you don't get any one area all soaked. The oil spray should be light, not heavy.

Be prepared to make a second batch! These will disappear fast, and I am not talking about magic tricks here.

INGREDIENTS:

- **Can of vegetable oil cooking spray**
- **12 corn tortillas**
- **Salt in a shaker**

YIELD: This recipe makes about 5 or 6 servings.

TIME: It takes about 30 minutes, start to finish.

YOU WILL ALSO NEED:

- Baking tray
- Scissors
- Serving bowl

ASK AN ADULT FOR HELP WITH:

- *Turning on the oven*
- *Putting the tray in the oven*
- *Helping decide when the chips are done*
- *Taking the tray out of the oven*
- *Taking the chips off the tray and putting them in a bowl*

1

Ask an adult to turn on the oven to 375°F.

Spray a baking tray with **oil spray**.

2

Make 6 piles of 2 **tortillas**. Use scissors to cut each group of tortillas into wedges or other fun shapes.

Try not to make them *too* tiny.

3

Spread all of the tortilla pieces (or as many as will fit) onto the tray. It's okay for them to touch and crowd a little, but they shouldn't pile up.

If you can't fit them all on the tray, you can bake a second batch.

4

Lightly spray the tortilla pieces all over with oil spray. (Hold the can about 12 inches away.)

4½

Sprinkle the tortilla pieces lightly with **salt**.

5

Ask an adult to put the tray in the oven for 10 to 12 minutes (until the chips are just right), and then to take it out.

6

Cool the chips on the tray for about 5 minutes, and then **ask an adult to put them in a bowl.**

TIME TO EAT!

Of all the green foods, this one might be the very best!

Guacamole is made from avocados, which are heavy, pear-shaped fruits that grow on trees. They are not sweet and juicy, like other fruit. Instead, they are thick and rich, with a gentle, quiet flavor. When you mash them up and add a few zesty seasonings, they make a great dip for tortilla chips (see Homemade Tortilla Chips on page 146). It's really fun to have some salsa on hand (see Real Salsa, page 154), so you can dip the chips into the guacamole and then into the salsa.

NOTE: Guacamole loses its color if it sits around for too long. Putting the avocado pits back in helps keep the color bright.

INGREDIENTS:

- **2 ripe avocados**
- **2 tablespoons freshly squeezed lemon juice**
- **$1/2$ teaspoon ground cumin**
- **$1/2$ teaspoon salt**
- **1 teaspoon minced (cut in tiny pieces) or crushed garlic**

YIELD: This recipe makes 5 or 6 servings.

TIME: It takes about 15 minutes, start to finish.

YOU WILL ALSO NEED:

- Citrus juicer
- Small, sharp knife and a cutting board (or garlic press) for mincing garlic
- Dinner knife
- Soup spoon
- Shallow dish for guacamole
- Fork
- Measuring spoons

ASK AN ADULT FOR HELP WITH:

- ***Slicing the avocados and taking out the pits***

1

Use a dinner knife to slice 2 **avocados** in half the long way (top to bottom). **You might need an adult to help.**

2

Open up the avocados and pull out the pits. **If that's too hard or messy, ask an adult to take out the pits with a small, sharp knife.** Save the pits.

3

Use a soup spoon to scoop out all of the soft, green insides. Put them in a shallow dish and mash them a little with a fork.

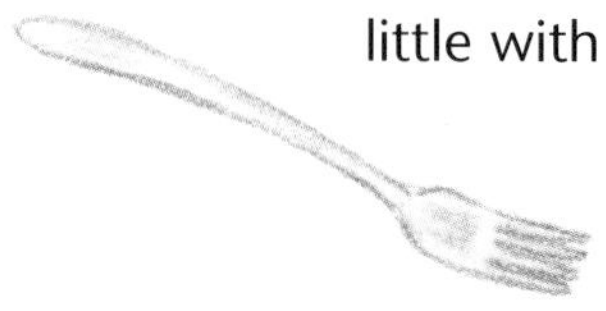

4

Add:

2 tablespoons **lemon juice**

$1/2$ teaspoon **cumin**

$1/2$ teaspoon **salt**

1 teaspoon **garlic**

5

Slowly mash in all of these ingredients until the guacamole is completely blended. (Be careful not to splash the lemon juice.)

If you are not going to serve it right away, put the avocado pits back in, cover the dish tightly with plastic wrap, and refrigerate. The pits will keep it from turning brown. Take them out before serving.

6

Serve with Homemade Tortilla Chips and Real Salsa.

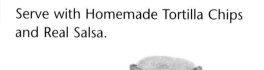

TIME TO EAT!

TWO-COLOR NACHOS

Nachos are very simple really: just a bunch of tortillas chips with cheese melted on them. But this recipe is special, because you use two different kinds of cheese—orange cheddar and white Monterey jack. It looks very pretty. It is even more special if you make these nachos with your own Homemade Tortilla Chips (page 146) and serve it with Real Salsa (page 154) and Hip Bean Dip (page 152). In fact, if you serve nachos with all of these yummy things, this snack could be lunch.

INGREDIENTS:

- **4 cups tortilla chips**
- **$1/4$ pound cheddar cheese**
- **$1/4$ pound white Monterey jack cheese**

YIELD: This recipe makes 3 or 4 servings.

TIME: It takes about 20 minutes, start to finish.

YOU WILL ALSO NEED:

- Baking tray
- Handheld grater or a food processor fitted with the grating attachment
- Timer with a bell
- Spatula
- Serving plate

ASK AN ADULT FOR HELP WITH:

- **Turning on the oven**
- **Helping grate the cheese, if using a food processor**
- **Putting the tray in the oven and taking it out**
- **Taking the nachos off the tray and putting them on a plate**

"Let's try to get the cheese all around the outside, because whenever I eat nachos, the outsides don't have any cheese." —Kyle

1

Ask an adult to turn on the oven to 350°F.

2

Spread the **tortilla chips** on a baking tray.

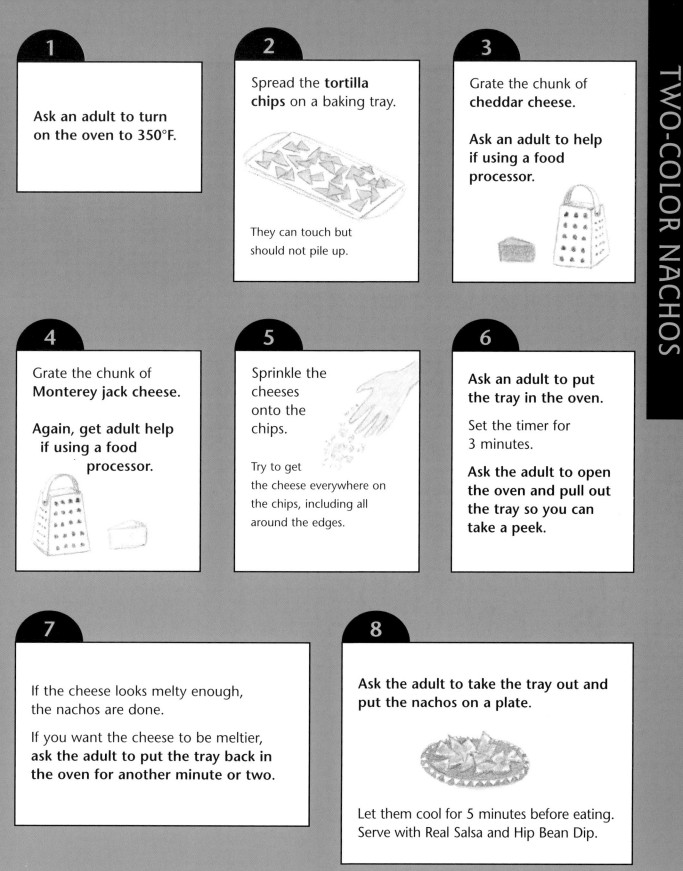

They can touch but should not pile up.

3

Grate the chunk of **cheddar cheese**.

Ask an adult to help if using a food processor.

4

Grate the chunk of **Monterey jack cheese**.

Again, get adult help if using a food processor.

5

Sprinkle the cheeses onto the chips.

Try to get the cheese everywhere on the chips, including all around the edges.

6

Ask an adult to put the tray in the oven.

Set the timer for 3 minutes.

Ask the adult to open the oven and pull out the tray so you can take a peek.

7

If the cheese looks melty enough, the nachos are done.

If you want the cheese to be meltier, **ask the adult to put the tray back in the oven for another minute or two.**

8

Ask the adult to take the tray out and put the nachos on a plate.

Let them cool for 5 minutes before eating. Serve with Real Salsa and Hip Bean Dip.

TIME TO EAT!

What is bean dip? Just beans that have been smushed up with seasonings, simple as that. Beans are very good for you. They have protein, vitamins, and fiber, all of which contribute to making your body strong and healthy.

Hip Bean Dip needs some decoration, because it comes out a gray color. This is easy to fix—just add a few leaves of deep green parsley and several strips of red bell pepper. It will look much brighter.

This tastes great with Homemade Tortilla Chips (page 146), or in a Bean Dip and Tortilla Chip Sandwich (page 50).

INGREDIENTS:

- 1 (15-ounce) can black beans, rinsed and drained
- 1 lime
- 1/2 teaspoon minced garlic (cut in tiny pieces)
- 1/4 teaspoon ground cumin
- 1/4 teaspoon salt
- 1/4 cup tomato juice or V-8 juice (optional)

EXTRAS FOR GARNISH (YOU CHOOSE):

- A few Italian (flat-leaf) parsley leaves
- A few strips of red bell pepper

YIELD: This recipe makes enough dip (about 2 cups) to serve 4 or 5.

TIME: It takes about 10 minutes, start to finish.

YOU WILL ALSO NEED:

- Can opener and wire-mesh strainer for opening and rinsing the beans ahead of time
- Food processor fitted with the steel blade
- Citrus juicer
- Measuring spoons
- Rubber spatula
- Serving bowl
- Sharp knife and a cutting board for preparing garnishes

ASK AN ADULT FOR HELP WITH:

- *Opening the can of beans and rinsing them off in a strainer*
- *Setting up the food processor*
- *Checking to see if the beans are mushed up enough*
- *Taking the bean dip out of the food processor*

152

1

Put the **beans** in the food processor.

2

Squeeze the juice from 1 **lime** with a citrus juicer. Measure 1 tablespoon **lime juice** and add it to the beans.

Save the rest of the lime juice, if there is extra, for your parents to use in something.

3

Also add:

1/2 teaspoon **garlic**

1/4 teaspoon **cumin**

1/4 teaspoon **salt**

4

Run the food processor until everything is totally mushed together.

Ask an adult to help check. If it seems a little stiff, you can add 1/4 cup **tomato juice** or **V-8 juice.** Buzz the food processor for another 2 seconds to mix it in.

5

Ask an adult to take the bean dip out of the food processor and put it in a bowl.

6

Decorate the dip with a few leaves of **parsley** and small strips of **red bell pepper** to give it some color.

7

Serve with chips or cut-up raw vegetables, or in a Bean Dip and Tortilla Chip Sandwich.

TIME TO EAT!

REAL Salsa

I can't think of a more adult thing for a kid to prepare than real salsa from fresh tomatoes. This is good stuff!

Serve it with Tortillas by Hand (page 87) or with Torn Tortilla Casserole (page 74). Or, just dunk some Homemade Tortilla Chips (page 146) in it and serve it along-side bowls of Guacamole (page 148) and Hip Bean Dip (page 152).

INGREDIENTS:

- 2 cups cherry tomatoes
- 2 scallions, minced (trim the "hairy" tip, and cut white and lower half of green part in tiny pieces)
- 4 fresh basil leaves
- 10 cilantro leaves
- Salt in a shaker
- 1 tablespoon red wine vinegar
- 1 tablespoon olive oil
- Hot sauce or Tabasco sauce (optional, and as much as you like)

YIELD: This recipe makes about 2 cups of salsa, enough for 4 to 5 people.

TIME: It takes about 15 minutes, start to finish.

YOU WILL ALSO NEED:

- Cup measure
- Small, sharp knife and a cutting board
- Medium-small bowl
- Scissors
- Measuring spoons
- Spoon for stirring

Should you ask an adult for help?

That's up to you, but make sure there is an adult in the house who knows you are doing this, has read through the recipe with you ahead of time, and can help you set up. (And, of course, if there is any task you feel uncomfortable doing, ask for help.)

1

Measure 2 cups **tomatoes.** Pull off their tops, and then carefully slice the tomatoes into tiny pieces and put them in a medium-small bowl.

2

Put the **scallions** in the bowl with the tomatoes.

3

Pile up 4 **basil leaves** and 10 small **cilantro leaves.** Snip them with scissors or cut them on a cutting board with a sharp knife until they are tiny. Put them in the bowl with the tomatoes and scallions.

4

Sprinkle in a few shakes of **salt.**

5

Measure 1 tablespoon **vinegar** and 1 tablespoon **olive oil,** and stir these in.

6

If you like it spicy, you can also add a few drops of **hot sauce** or **Tabasco sauce.**

7

Serve with Tortillas by Hand or Homemade Tortilla Chips, Torn Tortilla Casserole, Hip Bean Dip, or Guacamole—or all of these things at once!

TIME TO EAT!

CRUNCHY ZUCCHINI CIRCLES

It is very important that vegetables not be boring! Here is a great way to make zucchini interesting and exciting. You give each zucchini slice a tasty coating, and then cook it until it's crunchy on the outside but melty-tender inside. It's a snack food your parents will love for you to eat!

This is a fun project to make with friends. You can set up a production line, taking turns with the dipping and the cooking. You and your friends can munch on the circles while you are making more.

The first thing you do is slice some small zucchini into $1/4$-inch circles. Look at a ruler and memorize what $1/4$ inch looks like. Then, use the picture in your mind to cut the zucchini. Don't worry if the slices are not all exactly the same; some will be fatter and some will be skinnier, but they will all taste great!

After cutting the zucchini, you'll prepare a delicious batch of flavored bread crumbs. This is what makes the circles crunchy. One by one, you'll dip each zucchini piece in beaten egg and then into the bread crumbs, which stick to the egg. When you put the coated circles into the hot frying pan, the heat will toast the bread crumbs (just like the heat from a toaster toasts bread), and make them crunchy.

You can eat these hot, warm, or at room temperature.

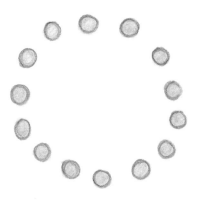

INGREDIENTS:

- 3 small zucchini (5 ounces each)
- 1 egg
- 2 tablespoons olive oil
- 6 tablespoons unseasoned fine bread crumbs
- 3 tablespoons grated parmesan cheese
- 1/4 teaspoon salt
- 1 teaspoon dried basil
- 1/2 teaspoon dried oregano
- 1/2 teaspoon onion powder

YIELD: This makes enough for 4 or 5 people to snack on.

TIME: It takes about 30 minutes, start to finish.

YOU WILL ALSO NEED:

- Small, sharp knife and a cutting board for preparing zucchini
- Small bowl for the egg
- Fork
- Measuring spoons
- Large frying pan
- Brush for painting the pan with oil
- Medium-sized bowl
- Plates for uncooked zucchini
- Spatula
- Plates and forks (or you can eat with your fingers)

ASK AN ADULT FOR HELP WITH:

- *Deciding if the oil is hot enough*

"Cut things so they are bite-sized. This means like a half or a quarter of your mouth." —Noah

1

Slice the 3 **zucchini** into circles about ¹/₄-inch thick on a cutting board.

2

Break an **egg** into a small bowl. Beat it with a fork until it is completely yellow and smooth.

3

Measure 2 tablespoons **olive oil** into a frying pan and brush it all around the inside of the pan.

4

Put the pan on the stove and turn on the heat to **medium.**

5

Measure into a medium-sized bowl:

6 tablespoons **bread crumbs**

3 tablespoons **parmesan**

¹/₄ teaspoon **salt**

1 teaspoon **dried basil**

¹/₂ teaspoon **oregano**

¹/₂ teaspoon **onion powder**

6

Mix until all of the ingredients in the bowl are combined. They will smell good!

7

Use a fork to hold a zucchini slice.

Dip the zucchini in the egg until it is wet, then dip it in the bread crumb mixture on both sides, until the crumbs stick to all of the surfaces of the zucchini. Do this to all the slices, putting them on plates as you go.

8

Ask an adult to help with this step.

Drop a bread crumb into the frying pan to see if the oil is hot enough yet. The bread crumb should sizzle a little.

9

Put the coated zucchini slices in the pan and cook for 5 minutes.

10

Turn them over with a spatula and cook on the other side for 5 more minutes.

11

Take the slices out of the pan with a spatula. Keep cooking until you have used up all of the zucchini.

12

Serve them hot, warm, or at room temperature.

TIME TO EAT!

GARLIC BREAD

Toasted garlic bread is always a big hit with kids *and* with grownups. It is really quite a simple idea: you toast some bread, then spread it with garlic-flavored butter and toast it again so the butter melts in.

To make garlic-flavored butter, you can use garlic powder, which is very easy because you just measure it out of a jar. Or you can mince fresh garlic to mix into the butter. Either way, this will taste great.

Whichever kind of garlic you decide to use, you will need to mash it into the butter, so the butter needs to be pretty soft. A good plan is to cut the butter about 30 minutes ahead of time, unwrap it, put it on a plate, and then leave it out of the refrigerator. It won't melt (unless it's a blazing hot day), but it will get warm enough to mash.

If you have any garlic-flavored butter left over, try putting some on cooked pasta, rice, or vegetables. (Mmmmm...It's great on cooked broccoli!)

YIELD: This recipe makes about 4 servings.

TIME: It takes about 50 minutes, start to finish (including time to soften the butter).

YOU WILL ALSO NEED:

- Small, sharp knife and a cutting board (or a garlic press) if using fresh garlic
- Dinner knife for cutting and spreading butter
- Dinner plate
- Bread knife
- Baking tray
- Timer with a bell
- Fork for smushing butter
- Measuring spoons

ASK AN ADULT FOR HELP WITH:

- *Turning on the oven*
- *Slicing the loaf in half*
- *Putting the tray in the oven*
- *Taking the hot bread off the tray and putting it back on*
- *Slicing the bread into servings*

INGREDIENTS:

- 6 tablespoons butter
- 1/2 pound loaf French or Italian (sweet or sourdough) bread
- 1 1/2 teaspoons garlic powder or 2 teaspoons minced (cut in tiny pieces) or crushed fresh garlic

160

1

Use a dinner knife to cut 6 tablespoons **butter.** Each line on the butter wrapper means 1 tablespoon.

Unwrap the butter, put it on a dinner plate, and let it get soft sitting at room temperature for about 30 minutes.

2

Ask an adult to turn on the oven to 375°F and to slice the loaf of bread in half the long way.

3

Put the 2 pieces of **bread** on a baking tray, cut side up.

Ask an adult to put the tray in the oven for about 8 minutes (until it is lightly toasted) and then to take it out.

4

While the bread is toasting, mash the butter with a fork until it is soft.

4¹/₂

Slowly sprinkle in 1¹/₂ teaspoons **garlic powder** or 2 teaspoons **fresh garlic.** Mash the butter some more and mix in the garlic.

5

Ask an adult to take the bread off the hot tray and stand by.

When the bread is not too hot to touch, spread the garlic butter all over the cut sides.

6

Ask an adult to put the bread back on the tray and the tray back in the oven for another 5 to 8 minutes (until toasty-perfect) and then to take it out and slice it.

TIME TO EAT!

Maple Yogurt Fruit Dip

Yogurt that comes already flavored is fun to eat. But sometimes it's also fun to flavor your own.

In this very simple recipe, you add real maple syrup to some plain yogurt. Once you stir it in, the syrup disappears, but you can really taste it. The sweetness of the maple syrup and the sourness of the yogurt go great together—and they taste absolutely wonderful scooped up with just about any kind of sliced fruit.

Try slicing up an assortment of your favorite seasonal fruits, like apples, bananas, oranges, pineapple, and pears in the winter, or melon, peaches, plums, cherries, and grapes in the summer. Put the fruit on a plate, and serve a bowl of Maple Yogurt Fruit Dip alongside for a perfect snack, or even for a light lunch on a warm day.

INGREDIENTS:

- 1 1/2 cups plain yogurt
- 4 tablespoons real maple syrup (or as much as you like)
- Slices of fruit for dipping (any kind)

YIELD: This recipe makes 5 or 6 servings, depending on the eaters and the time of day.

TIME: It takes about 5 minutes, start to finish (not counting time to cut the fruit).

YOU WILL ALSO NEED:

- Soup spoon
- 2-cup liquid measure
- Measuring spoons
- Whisk
- Spoon for tasting
- Small, sharp knife and a cutting board for slicing fruit
- Plate for the fruit
- Bowl for the yogurt
- Toothpicks

ASK AN ADULT FOR HELP WITH:

- *Slicing the fruit*

1

Spoon the **yogurt** into a 2-cup measuring cup until it reaches the line for 1¹/₂ cups.

2

Measure 4 tablespoons **maple syrup** and pour each tablespoon into the yogurt in the cup.

3

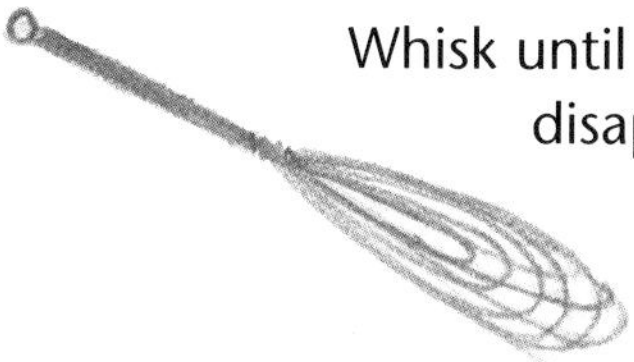

Whisk until the syrup disappears into the yogurt.

4

Take a little taste with a spoon. Is it sweet enough for you? If not, add a little more syrup.

5

Cut slices of your favorite **fruit**. **You might want adult help with this.**

Arrange the slices on a plate.

6

Pour the maple yogurt into a nice bowl and put it next to the plate of fruit. Put out some toothpicks to help with the dipping.

TIME TO EAT!

Summer Strawberry Treats

Here are two strawberry drinks that are very similar, except that one is thick and you scoop it with a spoon, and the other is liquidy. They are both whipped up in no time with ice cubes in a blender—quick and cold. *And* bright pink! One is *the* most refreshing thing in the world. And the other one is the *other* most refreshing thing in the world. Take your pick!

YIELD: Each recipe makes 1 or 2 servings.

TIME: Each takes about 10 minutes, start to finish.

YOU WILL ALSO NEED:

- Citrus juicer
- Blender
- Measuring spoons
- 1-cup liquid measure (for Liquado)
- 1 or 2 glasses (for Liquado)
- 1 or 2 small cups or bowls, and spoons (for Slush)

SLUSH INGREDIENTS:

- 20 fresh strawberries, stemmed and wiped clean
- 4 teaspoons freshly squeezed lemon juice
- 4 teaspoons sugar
- 10 to 12 ice cubes

LIQUADO INGREDIENTS:

- 20 fresh strawberries, stemmed and wiped clean
- 1/2 cup lowfat milk
- 1 tablespoon sugar
- 6 to 8 ice cubes

ASK AN ADULT FOR HELP WITH:

- ***Setting up the blender***

ICY STRAWBERRY SLUSH

1

Put in the blender:
- 20 **strawberries**
- 4 teaspoons **lemon juice**
- 4 teaspoons **sugar**
- 10 or 12 **ice cubes**

2

Blend until slushy and smooth.

3

Pour the slush into 2 small cups or bowls. Get out some spoons, and enjoy with a friend.

TIME TO SLURP!

STRAWBERRY LIQUADO

1

Put in the blender:
- 20 **strawberries**
- 1/2 cup **lowfat milk**
- 1 tablespoon **sugar**
- 6 or 8 **ice cubes**

2

Blend until slushy and smooth.

3

Pour into a glass.

TIME TO DRINK!

These two shakes are made with sorbet or frozen yogurt—and with lowfat milk (for the chocolate shake) or fruit juice (for the fruit shake). Since they are not too rich, you can drink them and not feel terribly full afterwards.

The amounts are very flexible in these recipes, which means you don't have to measure exactly. The chocolate shake, if made with sorbet, might need a little extra sugar. The fruit shake, on the other hand, might come out a little on the sweet side, and need some fresh lemon juice. Let your taste buds be your guide.

Here are some suggested flavor combinations for the fruit shake:

- Peach sorbet or frozen yogurt with cranberry juice

- Lemon sorbet or frozen yogurt in grapefruit juice

- Raspberry sorbet or frozen yogurt with orange juice

- Mango sorbet or frozen yogurt with lemonade

It tastes like air and like lemonade, only better. —Ariel

CHOCOLATE SHAKE INGREDIENTS:

- **Chocolate sorbet or frozen yogurt (about 3/4 cup per serving)**

- **Lowfat milk (about 1 cup per serving)**

- **1/4 teaspoon sugar (optional)**

FRUIT SHAKE INGREDIENTS:

- **Fruit-flavored sorbet or frozen yogurt— any kind (about 3/4 cup per serving)**

- **Fruit juice—any kind (about 1 cup per serving)**

- **1/2 teaspoon freshly squeezed lemon juice (optional)**

YIELD: Each of these recipes makes 1 or 2 servings.

TIME: Each takes about 10 minutes, start to finish.

YOU WILL ALSO NEED:

- 1 or 2 glasses

- Spoon for scooping sorbet or frozen yogurt and for stirring

- Blender

- Measuring spoons

- Citrus juicer for fruit shake

ASK AN ADULT FOR HELP WITH:

- ***Setting up the blender***

1

COOL & LIGHT
CHOCOLATE SHAKE

Put the **chocolate sorbet** or **frozen yogurt** in a glass. Fill it halfway.

2

Pour the **milk** into the glass until it comes up just a little bit higher than the sorbet or yogurt.

3

Pour it all into a blender. Blend until smooth. (Add a little more milk if it seems stiff.) Pour it back into the glass.

4

Taste it.
If it's not quite sweet enough, you can add about $1/4$ teaspoon **sugar**.

Stir and enjoy!

TIME TO DRINK!

1

COOL & LIGHT
FRUIT SHAKE

Put the **fruit sorbet** or **frozen yogurt** into a glass. Fill it halfway.

2

Pour the **juice** into the glass until it is just a little bit higher than the sorbet or yogurt.

3

Pour it into a blender. Blend until smooth. (Add a little more juice if it seems stiff.) Pour it back into the glass.

4

Taste it.
If it's too sweet, add $1/2$ teaspoon or so of **lemon juice.**

Stir and enjoy!

TIME TO DRINK!

Purple Passion POWER SHAKE

When you whip up this beautiful drink and take a few sips, you'll feel like you're bursting with energy!

This is so good for you, your parents might even let you drink it for breakfast. Or, try packing it up in a thermos and taking it to school to have with your lunch. It just might keep you feeling cheerful and powerful all day.

NOTE: This contains vanilla-flavored protein powder, which you can find at natural foods stores.

INGREDIENTS:

- 1/3 cup vanilla yogurt
- 1/4 cup blackberries or blueberries, fresh or frozen (optional)
- 1/2 ripe banana (optional)
- 1 tablespoon freshly squeezed lemon juice
- 1 cup unsweetened purple grape juice
- 1 tablespoon vanilla-flavored protein powder
- 2 ice cubes

YIELD: This makes 1 large serving or 2 smaller servings.

TIME: It takes about 10 minutes, start to finish.

YOU WILL ALSO NEED:

- Spoon
- 1-cup liquid measure
- Blender
- Citrus juicer
- Measuring spoons
- 1 or 2 glasses

ASK AN ADULT FOR HELP WITH:

- *Setting up the blender*

1

Spoon the **yogurt** into the measuring cup until it reaches the line for $^1/_3$ cup. Pour this into the blender.

2

If you like, you can add (either or both):

$^1/_4$ cup **blackberries** or **blueberries**

$^1/_2$ **banana**

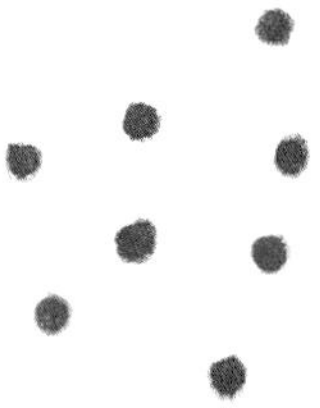

3

Squeeze a **lemon.** Measure 1 tablespoon **lemon juice** and pour this in.

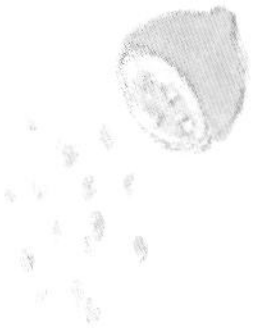

4

Measure 1 cup **grape juice** and pour it in.

5

Add:

1 tablespoon **protein powder**

2 **ice cubes**

6

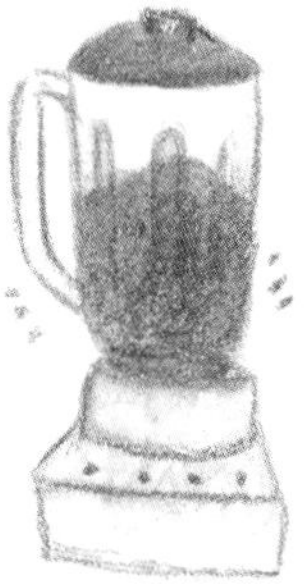

Blend until smooth.

Pour it into 1 or 2 glasses.

TIME TO DRINK!

HEALTHY SNACK IDEAS

HAPPY TRAILS MIX

Ask an adult to take you to a grocery store that has bins full of crunchy, munchy things, like nuts, raisins, and yogurt-covered treats. Say you'd like to create your own trail mix to nibble on between meals, or to put in your lunchbox for schoolday snacking. Then, pick out various things, keeping in mind that it's a good idea to use similar amounts of crispy, salty things (peanuts, soy nuts, cashews, almonds, sesame sticks, pretzels) and softer, sweeter things (dried apricots, cherries, cranberries, raisins). When you get home, open all of the plastic bags and pour the goodies into a big bowl. Gently mix them up and then scoop the colorful mix into individual, small, sealable plastic bags. Grab a pack whenever you need an energy-boosting snack. And you designed it yourself!

INSTANT FRUIT SORBET

It's really easy to make instant fruit sorbet. All you need is some frozen fruit, a little sugar, and a food processor. First, freeze some fruit. The kinds that work best are mangoes, melons, peaches, apricots, kiwis, strawberries, and pears. Take off the skin or peel (or remove pits, strawberry tops, watermelon seeds, or cores). Then, cut the fruit into chunks about an inch big, put them into plastic bags or lidded containers, close them up tightly, and freeze them. **Ask an adult to help.**

When the fruit is frozen, **ask an adult to set up the food processor with the steel blade.** Put in some chunks of frozen fruit and run the machine. If the fruit seems too hard, let it sit for 10 minutes, and then try again. In just a few minutes, you'll have a delicious slush! Taste to see if it is sweet enough, and stir in a little sugar if you like. **Ask an adult to take the sorbet out of the food processor,** and it's time to eat!

FROZEN FRUIT POPS

Make your own popsicles out of real fruit! This is how: Push popsicle sticks (available at arts-and-crafts stores) into pieces of peeled, soft fruit (like half a banana, chunky slices of mango, half a peach or apricot, a whole peeled kiwi, a large strawberry). Then, freeze the fruit-on-a-stick in a sealed plastic bag for a delicious, natural fruit "pop." These last longer than regular popsicles, which makes them great for long, warm summer afternoons. And there are no worries about getting sticky hands, because they don't drip.

"I like how everything tastes very delicious and refreshing."—Chelsea

EXCELLENT SODA

Most kids love store-bought soda, and, chances are you're going to drink it from time to time. But sometimes, when you're home, try making this healthy soda for yourself and your friends. It's fun and easy—and pretty friendly to your teeth and body, as well. Did I forget to say it tastes as good as (or maybe even *better* than) what you drink from cans or bottles? It truly does.

Here's the formula: For each serving of Excellent Soda, put 3 tablespoons of frozen juice concentrate in a cup. (Use any kind of concentrate you like—orange, apple, cranberry, cherry—whatever your parents have on hand.) Stir it around until it gets soft. Add $1/2$ cup sparkling water, stir it up, add an ice cube or two if you like, and you've done it. Time to drink!

VEGETABLE DIPS

Why is it that vegetables are so much more fun to eat when you get to dip them in something? Who knows. But it's true.

All of these pack up very easily for lunchboxes or after-school snacks:

- Ranch Dressing (a favorite!), page 58

- Hip Bean Dip, page 152

- Guacamole, page 148

This may sound strange, but another delicious and easy dip for vegetables is tomato sauce from a jar, the kind you put in lasagna or on spaghetti. You don't even have to heat it up—it tastes quite good cold on a piece of carrot or bell pepper.

After you've gotten the dip together, **ask an adult to help you slice some cucumbers, bell peppers, and celery to go with it.** Add some baby carrots and cherry tomatoes, and you're all set. And don't forget, olives can be considered a vegetable too, and they also taste incredible with any of the dips on this list.

LITTLE FRUIT AND CHEESE KEBABS

This is like an arts-and-crafts project that you can eat. Cut an apple and some cheese into small cubes. Have a handful of raisins and a few toothpicks ready. Make little apple, cheese, and raisin arrangements on the toothpicks in any order you like. (You can also use pineapple chunks, banana slices, or pieces of ripe pear.) Eat the kebabs pretty soon after you make them, when they're nice and fresh.

INDEX

BEST-SELLERS BY MOLLIE KATZEN...

MOOSEWOOD COOKBOOK
NEW REVISED EDITION

With well over 2 million copies in print, the *Moosewood Cookbook* is on The New York Times list of the top ten best-selling cookbooks of all time. Mollie Katzen's sophisticated, easy-to-prepare vegetarian recipes, charming pen-and-ink drawings, hand lettering, and conversational tone have converted millions to a more healthful, exciting way of cooking. This

new edition preserves the major revisions and additions that Mollie made in 1992, adding 5 new recipes from her current repertoire and 16 pages of beautiful color photography.

8 1/2 x 11 inches • 256 pages • paperback and hardcover

Coming January 2000

ENCHANTED BROCCOLI FOREST
NEW REVISED EDITION

The treasured second volume in Mollie Katzen's series features over 200 classic vegetarian recipes. First revised

in 1995, this new edition includes 5 new recipes and 16 pages of color food photography in addition to Mollie's intricate pen-and-ink drawings.

8 1/2 x 11 inches • 320 pages • paperback and hardcover

Coming January 2000

STILL LIFE WITH MENU
REVISED EDITION

Revised to accommodate lower-fat and easier-to-follow recipes (over 200 in all), this gorgeously illustrated full-

color cookbook presents complete vegetarian menus that range from the simple and comforting to the absolutely elegant.

8 1/2 x 11 inches • 256 pages • paperback

PRETEND SOUP
AND OTHER REAL RECIPES
A COOKBOOK FOR PRESCHOOLERS & UP

This delightful, award-winning "first cookbook" for preschoolers and up features 19 illustrated vegetarian

recipes and introduces numerals and a few easy-to-read words, allowing your child to move from the usual role of helper to head cook. Recipes are preceded by detailed set-up and safety instructions for the prep cook: the adult.

8 x 10 inches • 96 pages • hardcover

Available at your local bookstore, or order direct from the publisher.
To order, or for more information, call 1-800-841-BOOK.
Write or call for our free catalogs of books and posters.

TEN SPEED PRESS/TRICYCLE PRESS
P.O. Box 7123 • Berkeley, California 94707 • 1-800-841-BOOK • www.tenspeed.com